ɔ, Elisabeth.

ultural
dsł ip.

—

Intercultural Friendship

A Qualitative Study

Elisabeth Gareis

University Press of America, Inc.
Lanham • New York • London

Copyright © 1995 by
University Press of America,® Inc.
4720 Boston Way
Lanham, Maryland 20706

3 Henrietta Street
London, WC2E 8LU England

Library of Congress Cataloging-in-Publication Data

Gareis, Elisabeth.
Intercultural friendship : a qualitative study / Elisabeth Gareis.
    p.   cm.
Includes bibliographical references and index.
1. Students, Foreign--Social networks--United States. 2. Friendship--
Cross-cultural studies. 3. Cultural relations--Case studies.   I. Title.
    LB2376.4.G368   1995   302.3 ' 4--dc20   95-35626 CIP

ISBN 0-8191-9547-2 (cloth: alk: ppr.)

⊖™ The paper used in this publication meets the minimum
requirements of American National Standard for Information
Sciences—Permanence of Paper for Printed Library Materials,
ANSI Z39.48—1984

To my parents.

iii

Contents

List of Figures   vii

Preface   ix

Acknowledgments   xi

The Analytical Framework

Chapter 1   **Introduction**   1

Chapter 2   **U.S. Friendship Patterns**   7

Chapter 3   **Friendship Patterns of Other Cultures:
            Germany, India, and Taiwan**   25

Chapter 4   **Intercultural Friendship Formation**   47

The Case Studies

Chapter 5   **Setting and Background of Case Studies**   69

Chapter 6   **German-American Friendship Experiences:
            Five Case Studies**   77

Chapter 7   **Indian-American Friendship Experiences:
             Five Case Studies**   93

Chapter 8   **Taiwanese-American Friendship Experiences:
             Five Case Studies**   111

Chapter 9   **Case Study Results**   127

Chapter 10   **Implementations**   143

Appendices   149

Bibliography   165

Index   179

List of Figures

Figure 1. Factors Influencing the Formation of Intercultural   49
           Friendship

Figure 2. Relationship Between Contentment and Intimacy   129
           Needs in Intercultural Friendship Among Study
           Participants

Preface

In study after study, the lack of American friends emerges as one of the uppermost complaints foreign students have about their sojourn. Unfortunately, research on intercultural friendship in general and its culture-specific patterns is still rudimentary.

Due to the unexplored nature of the subject, this book uses a descriptive approach in an attempt to generate foundational information and lay the groundwork for more directed research. At its core are 15 case studies describing the actual friendship experiences of foreign students on a large U.S. campus.

In preparation for the case studies, the first four chapters provide an overview of the existing knowledge base on the subject. Chapter 1 introduces the reader to the promises and pitfalls of intercultural friendship and provides a definition of terms. Chapters 2 and 3 describe culture-specific friendship patterns in the U.S.A. and in the home countries of the case study subjects (Germany, India, and Taiwan). Chapter 4 delineates the factors involved in the formation of intercultural friendship formation.

Following this preliminary discussion, Chapter 5 introduces the setting and background for the case studies. Chapters 6, 7, and 8 then describe the actual friendship experiences of the 15 students, presenting anecdotes and the students' own insights, and suggesting culture-specific trends. Chapter 9 discusses the results of the case studies, comparing the actual friendship experiences with the previously reported status quo and analyzing them according to the factors influencing friendship formation presented in Chapter 4. Chapter 10 concludes by highlighting the findings and suggesting questions to be addressed in future research.

Acknowledgments

Acknowledgements are due to Dr. Tom Cooper and Dr. Genelle Morain for their encouragement and inspiration, to Dean Gordhan L. Patel at the University of Georgia for his support, to Mollie Brunson for her expert formatting and word processing skills, and to my husband Ryoya Terao for his nurturance, help, and unending patience.

Chapter 1

Intercultural Friendship: An Introduction

With the increasing availability of mass transportation in the last decades and the resulting internationalization of the world, a new field of study has been created and gained importance: intercultural communication. Still in its infancy, many aspects of intercultural communication are just beginning to be explored. One of these areas is intercultural friendship.

Be it in the course of travel, studies, business abroad, or immigration, prolonged contact between people from different cultures has only been greatly facilitated recently. Such contact holds the potential for many kinds of relationships, ranging from mere coexistence to the formation of close friendships. While there are plenty of examples for more or less peaceful coexistence and loose-knit associations, making close friends across cultures poses more of a challenge. The problem is that in intercultural friendships added dimensions have to be dealt with that do not exist in intracultural friendships. In intracultural friendships, variables such as values, interests, personality traits, and changes in circumstances concerning the individuals involved have to be juggled to create an often precarious balance. In addition to these problems, intercultural friendship has to cope with cultural differences--not the least of which is a discrepancy in the definition of friendship--and in most cases there also is the barrier of language between the interactants. The fact that some people are attracted to and interested in people from other cultures--maybe because of a fascination for the exotic--might help the first stages of friendship and supply motivation for its maintenance and development, but it does not eliminate problems specific to intercultural friendship.

Considering the growing interdependence of the world's cultures and the desirability of worldwide peace and understanding, the study of intercultural friendship is of utmost urgency. Maybe the area of intercultural contact with most impact on the future of international relations is the interaction of foreign and native students on the world's campuses. Here, young people from different countries meet each other. Since many of these individuals may be destined to fill influential positions and make decisions of far-reaching import later in their lives, campus friendships may prove to be extremely important for international relations. As Hull (1978, p. 103) notes, however, contact per se does not result in positive attitudes. Research findings agree that one of the conditions for positive attitudinal change following intergroup contact is intimate rather than casual contact (Gudykunst, 1979, p. 180; Yum, 1988, p. 765). This notion is corroborated by research done on foreign student satisfaction in the United States (U.S.). In study after study, the lack of American friends emerges as one of the uppermost complaints foreign students have about their sojourn (e.g., Hull, 1978, pp. 103-141). Not only does this condition affect the social life of their stay, it also is very strongly tied to their overall experience of success and their subsequent feelings toward the host society. Thus, as the presence of friendships with host nationals frequently contributes to a positive image, the absence thereof often results in negative evaluations of the country (Kapoor & Smith, 1978).

Unfortunately, the study of friendship in general has not been given due respect by the social sciences, resulting only in sporadic publications from the fields of sociology, anthropology, and psychology. By the same token, existing research on intercultural friendship patterns and particularly the intercultural friendship experiences of foreign students is rudimentary at best. As Furnham and Alibhai (1985, p. 710) note: "Very little has been done on the friendship networks and preferences of foreign students." Hull (1978, p. 185) states that when he asked the foreign student respondents of his study in the United States for suggestions on how to increase meaningful contacts with Americans, they could not come up with any that had not been "discussed in the literature and tried again and again in U.S. higher education." Assuming that he is referring to such measures as integrated housing, international clubs, international nights, and the like, it becomes clear that they provide commendable opportunities for contact but ultimately leave the interacting individuals on their own and helpless as to making the contact meaningful and intimate. At another place, Hull (1978, p. 106) notes that "no one has yet been able to measure the quality of contact [between foreign students and Americans]." We need to concentrate precisely on the quality of these contacts, however, to find out what does or does not make intercultural friendships work. Without this basic knowledge, attempts to improve the social side of foreign student programs on a small scale as well as moves to increase understanding between cultures on a large scale will be lacking an essential part of their foundation and will therefore be futile.

Definitions

Terminology concerning intercultural issues frequently meets with controversy. While some people like the term *foreign student*, for example, others feel it has a negative connotation and favor *international student* instead. Terminology is thus often a matter of personal preference. In this book, the following choices were made:

The term *intercultural* denotes situations involving two or more cultures and is used mainly to refer to relationships between people from two different cultural backgrounds. Since this book focuses on a qualitative study of intercultural friendship on a U.S. campus, most of the described intercultural relationships are thus between American students and foreign students from a variety of countries. The term *intercultural* is often used as a synonym for *cross-cultural* but favored here due to its convenient linguistic similarity to *intracultural*, alluding to matters within one culture.

No solution proves satisfactory concerning the choice between *country* and *culture*. As Hull (1978, p. 56) notes: "No one would want to argue too seriously that political boundaries are really representative of cultural groups, per se." Cultures can extend over country borders, and countries can comprise more than one culture. Since foreign students are officially grouped by their home countries, nationality was used as an identifier here. To elicit more detailed knowledge and create a more scientific basis for conclusions, however, a preliminary questionnaire that was distributed to all study participants contains an item about the region of origin within the home country and inquires whether the respondent identifies with a special cultural group.

The adjective *American* is used in a narrow sense referring to matters pertaining to the United States and to persons who have grown up in the United States and are fully acculturated. Even though *American* is a broad term and could be used to encompass North and South America and within each continent several nationalities, it is not meant to condescend or add an imperialistic flavor. It was selected merely to circumvent the problems connected with the other alternative terms and to prevent cumbersome circumlocutions. (The term *North American,* for example, would have included Mexicans and Canadians, and the term *U.S. citizen* could refer to newly arrived immigrants, not yet acculturated.) The term *foreign student* was chosen to identify college students studying in countries other than that of their citizenship. It is specifically used for non-American students enrolled at universities in the United States. *Foreign student* was selected in favor of *international student* because of its greater precision (Althen, 1983, pp. 140-141).

To define *friendship* would be, to say the least, a bold enterprise. Matthews (1986, p. 13), whose study on friendship is one of several thorough treatments of the subject that have come out of the United States in recent years, notes that

> [in the current literature,] the definition of a friend, the meaning of friendship to individuals, has rarely been the issue addressed. Most researchers have assumed that their own definition of friendship is shared by other members of society, rather than attending to the way respondents defined the term. The variety or ways of being a friend and the meaning attached to the word by various members of society and the same members at different times is largely unexplored.

While Matthews refers only to the definitional problem in the United States, the predicament is hardly alleviated when one includes friendship in other cultures. As Fahrlander (1980, p. 16) stresses: "The definition of 'friendship' varies from culture to culture with respect to spread, obligation, duration and mutual trust." As far as the United States is concerned, for example, the term *friend* is used "to describe a variety of relationships ranging from short-term superficial ones to long-standing ones to which the persons involved are deeply committed" (Matthews, 1986, p. 11). If we were to break this continuum into two rough categories, the terms *casual friend* and *close friend* may be juxtaposed. *Casual friends* may thereby be defined as associates bonded by sociability and *close friends* as showing closure toward the outside world and an added dimension of intimacy within the friendship (Rubin, 1985, p. 200; Bell, 1981, p. 22). Although this study concentrated more on close friendship, the respondents were free to elaborate on other levels of friendship if they wished. Considering the conceptual dilemma in general, they were not provided with a definition of friendship but asked to supply their own.

Chapter 2

U.S. Friendship Patterns

Until about a decade ago, the subject of American friendship patterns was neglected if not ignored by researchers in the applicable fields. Recent years, however, have seen an increase in works published on the topic, a fact attributed to a crisis in the family and the concurrent void in emotional, social, and intellectual need fulfillment (Rubin, 1985, p. 9). These publications examine the status quo of American friendship patterns from an intracultural, i.e., endemic and noncomparative perspective. They focus mostly on middle-class European Americans, but do delve into differences occurring during the various developmental stages of a lifetime, describe the effects of marital status on friendships, and contrast the typical friendship formations of men and women.

Most studies on American friendship patterns are qualitative in nature, deriving their information from in-depth interviews and questionnaires. The reason for this predominance of qualitative research is that definitions and experiences of friendship vary from person to person and through the course of each individual's life. As Matthews (1986, p. 22) states,

> research in which respondents are simply asked to identify their friends and then to answer questions about each one ignores these differences. The diversity of the meanings of friendship through the life course and

the variety of meanings represented by the informants can be discovered in qualitative research because the criteria used are revealed in discussion.

This propensity of friendship research for qualitative methods is the reason why quantitative treatments remain rare. Among the quantitative studies, the *Psychology Today* survey of 1979 (Parlee, 1979) is perhaps the most widely known. But even though the survey was extensive (over 40,000 readers responded), it has come under heavy criticism over the years. As Rubin (1985, pp. 199-200) notes, this criticism centers around two shortcomings. On one hand, the respondents were all readers of *Psychology Today* and therefore had special characteristics (e.g., 91% of the respondents were white, 53% never married, 68% between 18 and 34 years of age) (Parlee, 1979, p. 44). In addition, the sample was self-selected (e.g., 72% of the respondents were female) (Parlee, 1979, p. 44). Thus, the results of the survey are not as representative as they might seem. Even if samples of quantitative studies are more randomly selected, however, it is difficult to do justice to the descriptive nature of the subject matter.

The Meaning of the Word "Friend"

All studies have in common that at one point a definition of friendship is attempted. This definition usually contains three tiers: a reference to the degree of formalization of kinship and friendship ties, a delineation of relationship descriptors, and a listing of the functions and values of friendship.

Formalization

Most studies make a mention of the fact that friendship in the United States is not formalized. In many non-Western societies, friendship carries with it social rituals, public ceremonies, behavioral norms and a well-developed set of rights and obligations (Rubin, 1985, pp. 4, 8, 199). "Among the Bangwa of the Cameroon, for example, in a custom analogous to the arranged marriage, children are given a best friend by their parents, and the friends then assume lifelong commitments and obligations to each other" (Rubin, 1985, p. 199). In the United States, on the other hand, only kinship has such an institutional form. Friendship is voluntaristic; there are no friendship rituals or ceremonies, and existing behavioral norms, rights, and obligations are ambiguous and merely implied (Bell, 1981, p. 12).

Relationship Descriptors

A factor very much tied in with this ambiguity is the absence of linguistic forms to clearly delineate different kinds of relationships. Thus, the term *friend* is used to describe a variety of relationships ranging from short-term, superficial ones to ones that are long-standing and deeply committed (Matthews, 1986, p. 11). For the exacting language user, terms such as *acquaintance, casual friend, close friend,* and *best friend* offer the promise of a differentiation; however, even they have no clear demarcation, as is illustrated by Webster's equivocal definition of an *acquaintance* as "a person whom one knows but who is not a particularly close friend" (Webster's New Collegiate Dictionary, 1981, p. 52). To understand this definition, one would of course first have to know what a close friend is. Yet, the terms *close friend* as well as *casual, good, true, real,* or *best friend* are used with highly subjective variations and are largely unexplored in the research literature. This lack of definitive criteria makes it very difficult to differentiate among the terminology and, together with the beforementioned absence of formalization, to determine the existence of friendship (Matthews, 1986, p.25). It is under this premiss that Rubin (1985, p. 8) states:

> Without institutional form, without a clearly defined set of norms for behavior or an agreed-upon set of reciprocal rights and obligation, without even a language that makes distinctions between the different kinds of relationships to which we apply the word, there can be no widely shared agreement about what is a friend. Thus it is that one person will claim as a friend someone who doesn't reciprocate; that another who has been called a good friend says, when I ask him about his relationship, "Oh, yeah, John, we worked together a year or so ago. Haven't seen him since."

Despite the lack of established definitions, most studies focus on the description of what seems to correlate with best and close friendships, disregarding more casual relationships. One criterion for differentiation lies in numbers. Thus, when asked how many friends--meaning casual friends--they have, people respond with numbers as high as 30 to 50 (e.g., Matthews, 1986, p. 53). Close friendships, on the other hand, are fairly consistently limited to numbers between three and seven (e.g., Pogrebin, 1987, p. 10), and best friendships should by definition only include one person. To draw a more descriptive line between these three dimensions, we might utilize Du Bois' (1974, p. 20) interpretation of exclusive, close, and casual friendships. Thus, exclusive friendships are marked by a dyadic character, inclusive intimacy (i.e., confidences and responsibilities), and assumed permanence; close friendships occur in multiple dyads with selective intimacy and hoped-for durability; and casual friendships are polyadic, with incidental intimacy, and an unstressed attitude toward durability. For the sake of a common ground, this delineation will serve as a guideline here, and the term *friend* will predominantly be used to signify close and best friendships.

Functions and Values

Despite the definition problems, research findings widely agree on the functions and values of friendship. To introduce the discussion of functions and values, most studies list the elements necessary to induce the formation of friendships. The elements are proximity, homophily, reciprocal liking, and self-disclosure (e.g., Pogrebin, 1987, pp. 56-65). It should be added that the first of these elements, proximity, means (at least initial) face-to-face contact in most cases; in literate societies, however, friendships may at times be initiated and maintained exclusively through written communication (Du Bois, 1974, p. 21). Of the elements necessary for the formation of friendship, homophily is the single most important one. According to Dodd (1991, pp. 229-238), the word *homophily* is used to describe similarities among persons with regard to appearance (looks, size, even clothing), age, education, residence, social class, economic situation, social status, personality traits, opinions, attitudes and values. To differentiate between the latter

two, attitudes are more numerous, specific in content, and peripheral to
an individual's personality; whereas values are more encompassing and
central, referring to a person's weltanschauung (Yang, K. S., 1986, p.
126). Matthews (1986, p. 12) adds gender, race, and marital status; and
Bell (1981, p. 19) also includes interests and intelligence as variables.

The reasons why similarity plays such an essential role in the
formation of friendship are manifold; however, they all are connected
with one of the major functions of friendship, to provide reassurance of
identity. This reassurance applies to the general sense of self-worth
(Bell, 1981, p. 15); it can be employed eclectically by selecting diverse
friends, each meeting different parts of ourselves; it can be used to affirm
new roles and give them an internal reality (e.g., the formation of
friendships with married people once somebody enters wedlock affirms
the shift from single to married life); it can help us realize our aspirations
if the friend is a role model and by his or her example propels us beyond
our preconceived limits; and it can be central in the maintenance of our
sanity if we are outside the mainstream of society and by virtue of a
social, demographic, or political factor are subject to prejudice and
discrimination (Rubin, 1985, pp. 40-43, 48-54, 56, 181). In connection
with homophily, two American proverbs come to mind: "Opposites
attract" and "birds of a feather flock together." While opposites might
attract at times, either to fill personality voids, complement needs, or to
reflect one's dormant characteristics wanting expression, most of the
time friendship thrives on similarity (Progrebin, 1987, p. 58), and a
closer look at some outwardly disparate pairings reveals likeness in
crucial aspects of the friends' make-up.

Besides homophily and the ensuing reassurance of identity, four other
groups of functions can be condensed from the myriad of mentioned
attributes. The first group may be called *affection* and comprises notions
such as reciprocal liking (Pogrebin, 1987, pp. 60-63), love, (Parlee,
1979, p. 43), intimacy (Matthews, 1986, p. 13), and other emotional
rewards (Pogrebin, 1987, pp. 23). The second group of friendship
functions may be termed *support* and appears as crisis support (Bell,
1981, p. 19), assistance (Matthews, 1996, p. 13), protection (Du Bois,
1974, p. 16), security (Pogrebin, 1987, p. 23) or safety (Rubin, 1985, p.
181) in the research literature. This support function of friendship may
necessitate self-disclosure of problems, aspirations, and feelings which

many   social scientists see as the key to the formation of close friendships (Berman, Murphy-Berman, & Pachauri, 1988, p. 62). The third functional group is *gregariousness,* meeting our needs for sociability (Berman, Murphy-Berman, & Pachauri, 1988, p. 63), inclusion (Alter, Klopf, & Cambra, 1980, p. 7), affiliation (Bond & Hwang, 1986, p. 257), or community (Pogrebin, 1987, p. 21). Finally, *status and power* (Matthews, 1986, p. 13) are mentioned as functions of friendship, and similar concepts that would fall into this category are social prestige, economic advantage (Du Bois, 1974, p. 16) and instrumental rewards (Pogrebin, 1987, p. 23). Whereas the functions of identity reassurance, affection, support, and gregariousness rarely cause dispute, the last component of status and power is more controversial. Many studies, for example, mention the writings of Aristotle who differentiates between perfect friendships in which friends "desire the good of one another" (Aristotle, 1953, p. 233) and pleasant or useful friendships in which "the friend is not loved for being what he [she] is in himself [herself] but as the source, perhaps of some pleasure, perhaps of some advantage" (Aristotle, 1953, p. 232). Thus, if the purpose of the friendship is to gain status and power or even just pleasure, the friendship cannot be considered good. Good friendship automatically brings with it both pleasant and useful values, but is not based on them (Paine, 1974, p. 4). Pogrebin (1987, pp. 22-24) mirrors this distinction in what she calls *communal theory* and *exchange theory.* Communal theory says that the friend him- or herself is the reward and that real friends give to make each other happy, not to get something back. Exchange theory, on the other hand, stipulates that friendships require an exchange of resources and exist only as long as equal benefits can be derived; these benefits may include love but also comprise status, goods, money, and information. In a parallel motion, Du Bois (1974, p. 20) uses the terms *expressive* versus *instrumental* to differentiate between friends of virtue and friends of pleasure or utility. Both Du Bois and Cohen (1961b, pp. 352-353) then employ these concepts to claim that with increasing materialism, intimacy decreases and friendships slide on the continuum from exclusive to close to casual and purely expedient, thus deviating further and further from Aristotle's prototype of the perfect friendship.

Inseparable from the functions of friendship are the values desired in a friend. It is indeed sometimes difficult to differentiate between these two categories. To clarify the point, functions can be defined as fulfilling a purpose whereas values are more static qualities that human beings possess. It is under this premiss that affection and support can be grouped with the functions while the often-mentioned qualities of warmth and supportiveness (e.g., Parlee, 1979, p. 49) fall under the category of values.

Respondents in U.S. friendship studies are fairly unanimous concerning traits to be valued in a friend. The qualities most frequently mentioned are trust, honesty, and loyalty, followed by mutuality, generosity, warmth, supportiveness, and acceptance (e.g., Bell, 1981, p. 16; Matthews, 1986, p. 26; Parlee, 1979, p. 49; Pogrebin, 1987, pp. 36-44; Rubin, 1985, p. 7). At times, other values are mentioned in the research literature; at a closer look, however, they are very similar or practically synonymous with the qualitites mentioned above. Rubin (1985, p. 7), for example, lists commitment and constancy as heralded qualities of friendship; the more frequently used concept and the term used here is *loyalty,* which includes commitment and constancy. In the same vein, frankness (Parlee, 1979, p. 49) is covered by the preferred term *honesty,* flexibility (Matthews, 1986, p. 26) can be grouped under the category *generosity,* and the concept of *acceptance* serves as an umbrella for understanding and forgiveness mentioned by Rubin (1985, p. 7) and Bell (1981, p. 18).

Female and Male Friendship Styles

In any discussion of friendship, it has to be mentioned that a listing of functions and values as the one above can only be a generalization, with the specifics varying from individual to individual and even in the course of each person's life (Bell, 1981, p. 17). Besides this predictable personal variation, however, research literature also shows that there are noticeable differences between the sexes as a whole.

Women's Friendships

Women's friendships are usually described as expressive, confirming, and holistic with a predominance of talking over activities, dyads over group relationships, and high levels of intimacy, self-revelation, and nurturance (e.g., Bell, 1981, pp. 55-94, Mitchell, 1986, pp. 96, 145; Rubin, 1985, pp. 60-79). Research findings also agree that close friendships between women are more frequent than between men (e.g., Bell, 1981, pp. 63-64; Rubin, 1985, p. 60). These attributes often result in value judgements of women's friendships as deeper, richer, and more meaningful than men's friendships (e.g., Pogrebin, 1987, p. 253), a perception diametrically opposed to historical beliefs and portrayals in fictional literature where the models of friendship have been, with few exceptions, about men and for men (Bell, 1981, p. 58). Bell (1981, pp. 58, 60) explains this dichotomy:

> The "traditional wisdom" about female friendships has been to see them as inferior to those of men. This undoubtedly has been a reflection of a more general notion of female inferiority. If women are seen as inferior, then obviously what they do in most areas, including friendship, by definition will be inferior. Both women and men have often accepted this belief and downplayed women's friendships. . . . I would argue that the historical beliefs in the inferiority of female friendships are wrong. The evidence clearly indicates that the friendships of women are more frequent, more significant, and more interpersonally involved that those commonly found in men.

Rubin (1985, p. 60) agrees with Bell but adds that the traditional views are changing and that in literature "now, instead of lyrical tributes to the glory of male friendships, we have laments about men's problems with intimacy and vulnerability, about the impoverishment of their relationships with each other--at least among heterosexual men."

Men's Friendships

As can be almost inferred from the above comments, friendships among men are usually described as group-oriented, competitive, defined by roles (i.e., friends are seen as tennis partners, drinking partners, etc. rather than holistically), and emphasizing activities over talking; not surprisingly, playing or watching sports are an important part in many male friendships (e.g., Bell, 1981, pp. 55-94; Mitchell, 1986, pp. 99, 145; Rubin, 1985, pp. 60-79). Male friendships have been found to provide more continuance than female friendships (Costa, 1983, p. 72; Mitchell, 1986, p. 96), but they are also said to lack in affection, intimacy, and nurturance (e.g., Bell, 1981, pp. 55-94; Pogrebin, 1987, p. 254; Rubin, 1985, pp. 60-79). Thus, preferred topics among male friends are sports, work, and politics; the preferred mode of communication joking (Rubin, 1985, pp. 60-79). Feelings are rarely shared except when drinking has loosened restraints or in the form of joke insults (e.g., one man might call his friend a *cheap bastard* but mean it affectionately) (Bell, 1981, pp. 81-83; Rubin, 1985, pp. 71-72). Summarizing the negative press male friendship has received, Brown (1986, p. 10) calls it "one of the disaster areas of American life."

This rather harsh verdict concerning male friendships is softened in the research literature by several qualifying statements. Thus, the pattern seems widespread and not only restricted to the United States. Social scientists have consistently found that friendships in Western cultures in general are more frequent, more meaningful, and more involved among women than men (e.g., Berman, Murphy-Berman, & Pachauri, 1988, p. 61). One also has to keep in mind that the findings are generalized and do not necessarily apply to particular individuals or male subgroups; homosexuals, for example, generally exhibit quite different patterns (Rubin, 1985, pp. 149-174).

Researchers also ameliorate the judgement by furnishing explanations for the perceived deficiences. Thus, it is purported that men are very early socialized into a competitive mode by participation in team sports, and that this mode precludes the formation of close and loving relationships. Rubin (1985, p. 81) states that "it is not likely that they [youngsters] can put on a show of invincibility during the game and share their fears and vulnerabilities after it." The situation can be extrapolated to work in adult life. Since work usually is a major focus in men's lives and since it is competitive, to reveal weaknesses, failures, and worries openly would be to admit one's inferiority and risk disadvantages (Berman, Murphy-Berman, & Pachauri, 1988, p. 62).

Again, this competitiveness is so pervasive that it is not limited to work or sports but has become an integral part of many men's lives in general. The only exceptions, according to Brown (1986, p. 11) are circles at the very bottom and the very top of the social and economic ladder. Thus, for blue collar workers as well as inheritors of great wealth, group and class solidarity is more important than competition and may also encourage solidarity in friendships. Another traditional societal stipulation has been that men are strong, silent, individualistic, and control, channel, or repress their feelings; no wonder then that in communication between men, intensely personal subjects are avoided or reshaped into abstract general questions (Bell, 1981, p. 79; Berman, Murphy-Berman, & Pachauri, 1988, p. 62). In the same vein, research literature mentions homophobia as a deterrent for self-revelation; friendships are to reassure masculinity, and since emotional intimacy is seen as a feminine trait, it represents a threat to many men (Bell, 1981, pp. 79, 83). Rubin adds another reason for the lack of verbality concerning men's feelings by stating that in a boy's development, his separation from the mother and establishment of his male identity comes before his linguistic ability is formed sufficiently to express the resulting emotions; and it is this internal split between his lack of words and his feelings that causes the difficulties in bringing both together even later in life (Rubin, 1985, pp. 95-97).

Besides these explanations, a future projection serves to brighten up the status quo of male friendships. As manifested by a myriad of articles in popular magazines and the appearance of men's support groups, recent years have seen a trend for men towards more compassion, aesthetic interests, and expression of feelings (Bell, 1981, p. 92). If this trend continues, we will soon see an increase in more private and intimate types of relationships not only among friends but also within the family.

Cross-Gender Friendships

Closely related to the status quo of female and male friendship styles are research findings concerning friendships between women and men. Across the board, cross-gender friendships are described as different from same-sex friendships and not as frequent (e.g., Matthews, 1986, p. 102; Parlee, 1979, pp. 50, 53).

Among the reasons for this phenomenon is the abovementioned discrepancy in friendship styles. The greater nurturance and intimacy on the female end of the spectrum has several effects. For one, many men report that their closest friendships are with women, thus taking care of emotional needs not readily fulfilled in male friendships (Rubin, 1985, p. 98). Women, however, rarely share those men's perceptions. Rubin (1985, p. 1959) found that "about two thirds of the women who were named by a man as a close friend disavowed that definition of the relationship. Most acknowledged the friendship but did not count it as a close or intimate one." Only few women in Rubin's study put male friends in a class with close female friends, and all purported that those particular men were more like women (Rubin, 1985, p. 159). It is for the same reason that the above comments seem to apply largely to heterosexual men; close friendships between women and homosexual men are relatively common where these two come to know each other (Rubin, 1985, p. 171).

This bonding between women and gay men can be accounted for by a similarity in friendship styles but also by another affinity. Thus, women frequently refer to a sense of equality in their relationships with gay men (Rubin, 1985, p. 172). Since both groups have been discriminated against and devalued in the world of heterosexual men, their alliance seems a natural one (Rubin, 1985, p. 173). At the same token, friendships between women and heterosexual men do not come easy. As Pogrebin (1987, p. 316) states: "Male-female friendship is still the exception because equality--social equality--is still the exception." Yet, as men must learn to see women as full human beings, women must also accept men as people with feelings before true friendships can develop (Pogrebin, 1987, p. 316).

Another reason for the difficulties in cross-gender friendships is also societal. Even though members of both sexes are allowed to associate freely in the United States and sex differences are not maximized, cross-gender friendships are not actually encouraged (Du Bois, 1974, pp. 28-30; Parlee, 1979, p. 53). The reason for this reservation is no doubt moralistic, serving as a precaution against sexual involvement outside of marriage.

Indeed, the fact that sexual tension can rarely be eliminated from cross-gender friendships is considered a given in the research literature (e.g., Pogrebin, 1987, p. 319). It, at the very best, can add a certain flirtatious quality and vitality to a relationship or end in sexual involvement which often destroys the friendship on account of the frequently ensuing possessiveness and demands for exclusivity (Rubin, 1985, pp. 153-157). Matthews (1986, p. 100) implies that the few occasions in which sexual overtones can be excluded, are when the relationship could be compared to a familial one (for example, where there is a large age discrepancy) and when for some reason the friend can be ruled out as a potential lover or marriage partner.

Friendship Types

Besides the differences between female and male friendship styles, research literature sporadically also lists variations caused by individual propensities and preferences. Mitchell (1986, pp. 181-186), for example, found four prevalent friendship types in a quantitative study on adult friendships. The first type is labeled *expressive-confirming*, encompassing friendships that focus on conversation rather than activity and that are usually maintained during separation and change. The second cluster is called *active-affirming* and is characterized by activity and external affirmation of skills, behavior, and progress. The third type is named *possessive-ambivalent;* individuals with this disposition tend to find separation or changes difficult and show a high level of jealousy. The last pattern is termed *competitive-accepting*, and friendships in this cluster are marked by both shared activities and conversation, and a high level of conflict resolution.

Whereas Mitchell describes friendship types more statically, emphasizing affinities, Matthews (1986, pp. 33-58) in a study using oral biographies of senior citizens focuses on friendship patterns emerging over a life course. Three personality types are distinguished and labeled *independent, discerning*, and *acquisitive*. Matthews' respondents that were grouped in the independent category did not acknowledge ever having had close friends. Their contacts are friendly relations rather than friendships. Since independents focus on the present, they do no feel the necessity of a commitment for maintaining those relations after separation or life turnings. Yet, independent informants are not isolated or unhappy; they usually know many people, but these others appear more like an undifferentiated mass than individuals with whom close ties are to be established. Respondents classified as discerning, on the other hand, made clear distinctions between friends and friendly relations. For people in this category, close friendships are very important and are usually maintained throughout life. Discerning individuals do not have many of these close friends; and with a focus on the past, they are likely to stand alone in old age because as these few friends die away, they are not replenished. By contrast, acquisitive individuals collect a variety of friendships throughout life. Some of these friendships are long-term, some short-term; but they all are close and committed, at least for the duration of geographical proximity. In addition to having past and current friends, acquisitive people look to the future as well and make a conscious effort to add new friends, usually at turning points in life.

Life Changes and Friendship Duration

In the discussion of friendship types, the concept of life changes or turnings emerges time after time. These turnings, on one hand, include the typical developmental stages of infancy, childhood, adolescence, young adulthood, middle adulthood, and old age, each of them with inherent shifts of focus (e.g., Bell, 1981, pp. 31-54; Matthews, 1986, p. 151; Rubin, 1985, pp. 110-111). Turnings also comprise general significant events occurring in individuals' lives, such as college entrance, graduation, moves, changes in marital status, job changes, deaths of parents, retirement, etc. (e.g., Matthews, 1986, p. 33). Since the external changes at these turning points frequently ensue in internal changes (Rubin, 1985, p. 34), they play an important role in the formation and duration of friendships.

A turning in life usually means that new friendships are formed, either as additions to or replacements of old ones (Matthews, 1986, pp. 59-80).

Some individuals find it easy to maintain old friendships and merely add new ones throughout life changes. One reason for this continuance might be the superior quality of a particular friendship, assuming that good friendships are lasting while others are short-lived (Paine, 1974, p. 2). It might also reflect on the perceptive abilities of the individuals involved. As Du Bois (1974, pp. 26-27) notes, "persons whose perception of others is well-developed and accurate will form close friendships whose expected and actual duration coincide, whereas persons (of whatever age) whose perception is faulty, are more likey to have labile friendships." Another factor to be considered when discussing long-lasting friendships is that some friendships are perfunctorily maintained simply because they have existed for a long time (Bell, 1981, p. 24). These friendships often are little more than memories of the past. Even if the individuals profess that they can pick up their friendship after several years as if they had parted only yesterday, they might be able to do so only because the contact is limited. At a closer look, they may find that in fact they do not have enough in common any longer to sustain a more extended relationship (Bell, 1981, p. 69).

In the cases when friendships end at turnings, it is because the friends have changed in different directions (Rubin, 1985, p. 23), and the personalities have become so divergent as to inhibit the confidence and intimacy necessary for the continuation of close ties (Du Bois, 1974, p. 26). This termination is further facilitated by the absence of institutionalization of American friendships (Matthews, 1986, p. 74; Rubin, 1985, p. 186). Not all friendships need the rationale of a turning to end, however. As Brown (1986, p. 12) bleakly puts it, some friendships are terminated with the drying up of a single common interest. He states that many friendships in the United States are a "series of times together into which topics are stuffed, and when the topic has fallen flat or the available topics have been exhausted, the relationship becomes boring" and is often discarded.

When friendships end, they might do so in different ways. Pogrebin (1987, pp. 93-94) identifies three types of endings for friendships: baroque, classical, and romantic. Baroque endings are described as bombastic and high-flown; classical endings are rational, discussed between the friends, and attempting good taste; and romantic endings fade out with the understanding that facts might be too distressing to confront. Rubin (1985, p. 34) details that most friendships do go out in a whisper and not a bang, with individuals simply losing sight of one another and unceremoniously disconnecting.

Intercultural Views on American Friendship Patterns

When American friendship patterns are examined intraculturally, in isolation--as it was done in the previous section--the following summarized picture emerges: American friendships are not formalized; although the term *friend* is broad and applies to many different kinds of relationships, the number of close friendships is limited; homophily, affection, support, trust, honesty, and loyalty are oftmentioned elements of friendship; female and male friendship styles differ in degree of intimacy and other respects, and cross-gender friendships are complicated by issues of sexuality; individuals differ in their affinity for various friendship types (e.g., independent, discerning, and acquisitive); and life turnings frequently go hand in hand with changes in friendships or even their ending. While this internal picture provides insights, it offers only a one-sided perspective. For a more well-rounded examination, interculturally oriented texts furnish relativity and thus illuminate the subject matter further.

These intercultural publications include on one hand manuals for foreign student advisors (e.g., Althen, 1983) and a myriad of academic books and reports about foreign students on U.S. campuses (e.g., Du Bois, 1956; Hull, 1978). Besides these publications for administrators and academicians, materials are also available for the actual sojourners. Thus, almost all universities with a foreign student population supply handbooks geared to inform and orient incoming students (e.g., The University of Iowa Office of International Education and Services, 1991). In addition, a number of general interest books are on the market introducing American culture to not only students but also business personnel, immigrants, tourists, and other interested parties (e.g., Althen, 1988; Lanier, 1981; Stewart, 1972).

Among the variety of topics covered in these publications there are always sections on personal relations or friendship, and they almost verbatim reiterate the same message: Americans are friendly and warm during initial contact, but close friendships are either extremely rare or, if they do happen, are usually less intense and short-lived.

Some publications elaborate on this blanket statement by adding details or examples. Thus, it is frequently mentioned that Americans have difficulties in forming close friendships in general, not just across cultures (Althen, 1988, p. 78; Du Bois, 1956, p. 94; Stewart, 1972, p. 49). It is added that Americans tend to keep personal feelings and thoughts to themselves, that when socializing, they prefer doing activities together rather than just sitting and talking (Althen, 1988, pp. 26, 78), and that they frequently compartmentalize their friends into friends at work, friends at school, tennis friends, etc. (The University of Iowa Office of International Education and Services, 1991, p. 48). Another noted characteristic is that Americans avoid commitment and obligation (Stewart, 1972, p. 49). Two examples might be listed here. One is that foreigners often feel they cannot call Americans freely or ask them for help. The other example is that Americans may be very hospitable and easily invite foreigners into their homes, but that no strings are attached to that gesture, a fact which baffles the visitors who either think they have to reciprocate or who see the invitation as the sign of a budding close friendship (Lanier, 1981, p. 64).

To what extent this mosaic represents the intercultural status quo of American friendship patterns is open to questioning. Many of the details mentioned remind the reader of idiosyncratic, nongeneralizable aspects of American friendship. Thus, low self-disclosure, a preference for activities over talking, and compartmentalization of friends have been ascribed more to male than female friendship styles; and the lack of commitment and permanence are more characteristic of the independent and in part acquisitive friendship types than of discerning personalities. Nevertheless, the abovementioned picture *is* the one used to generalize about American friendship in the interculturally oriented literature, and the one recognized by many international visitors.

With this picture as a given, the biggest problem seems to be that initial displays of friendliness on the part of the Americans or gestures such as invitations to one's home are often misinterpreted as signaling the desire for a close friendship, and many foreigners feel betrayed when this perceived promise is not fulfilled (Paige, 1991, p. 48). A similar situation of disappointment arises when friendships are actually formed but then quickly fade as the American party moves or undergoes other life changes. It comes to no surprise that frustrated foreigners often conclude that American relationships are superficial in nature (e.g., Althen, 1988, p. 78).

In an attempt to aid the foreign visitors' understanding of American friendship patterns, intercultural publications often supply rationales for points of contention. Du Bois (1956, pp. 62-63, 93), for example, very generally cites that at least some constituents of friendship are culturally determined, and gives an example by mentioning that U.S. friendships are marked by high spread, low obligation, low duration, and high trust; in other words, American friendships tend to be widespread and trusting, but lacking in a sense of obligation and permanence. She cautions Americans about entering relationships with persons from high-obligation and high-duration cultures since it is in such relationships that American openness and friendliness are often ethnocentrically interpreted as promises of closer involvement, and a sense of disappointment and failure ensues on the part of the foreigners when this promise does not become realized. From another angle, Du Bois warns that the proverbial American friendliness might "appear to foreigners as a tactless intrusion into cherished areas reserved for close relationships" (Du Bois, 1956, p. 62) and is, therefore, doubly problematic. Du Bois also notes that the role of interpersonal relations in a culture in general needs to be analyzed. In the United States, for example, the emphasis is more on material well-being than relationships, placing a lower value on interpersonal relations in general than in some other cultures. On a narrower scale, we must also give attention to the degree of importance assigned to friendships *within* the hierarchy of these interpersonal relations and take into account cultural or individual discrepancies to avoid frustrating experiences.

Besides these universally applicable pointers, publications also list more concrete reasons based on U.S. history and American national traits. Thus, the high spread and compartmentalization of friendships is explained by Stewart (1972, p. 58) as a function of the wish to be popular; he purports that popularity and friendship are "matters of social success and not the conditions for establishing warm, personal relationships." Stewart (1972, p. 54) also supplies a reason for the perceived unavailability or inconvenienced reaction of Americans when it comes to assisting others. He states that Americans in need of help, support, or solace frequently search for professional help rather than make demands on friends. The most prominent explanation for the fear of close involvement and the lacking sense of commitment and obligation given in the literature, however, is the American ideal of independence and self-reliance. Research has shown that, when asked about values, Americans rank freedom first, well ahead of friendship (The Connecticut Mutual Life Report on American Values in the '80s, cited in Pogrebin, 1987, p. 9), an attitude leading to understandable caution with people who do want to get closely involved (Althen, 1988, p. 26). Another reason for the fear of involvement and simultaneously for the perceived short duration of American friendships can be found in American mobility patterns. Having grown up in families that might have changed their residence every few years, many Americans have either not had sufficient practice in forming close friendships or have developed self-protective habits of keeping relationships casual in order not to get hurt upon the repeated separations (Bell, 1981, p. 38). When turnings in adult life are also accompanied by frequent moving, chances for friendships surviving become slim. American historic mobility patterns do not match ideals of commitment, responsibility, obligation, and permanence; the result is that people have learned to develop instant intimacy but also to let go quickly and with ease (Rubin, 1985, pp. 196-197).

Chapter 3

Friendship Patterns of Other Cultures: Germany, India, and Taiwan

One of the premisses of intercultural research is that the observer is confronted with the sociolinguistic problem of defining the divergent meanings of analogous terms. This predicament naturally also exists and might be the core in friendship research. Even though there may be universals that apply to friendship across cultures (possibly in such traits as affection, support, trust, and honesty), many elements taken for granted in one culture are negated in others. For example, homophily might be passed over by assigned friendships and voluntarism denied by the formalized arrangements common in some cultures. Thus, the connotations attached to the term *friendship* may vary across cultures from mere subtleties to great amplitudes. Unfortunately, literature on friendship patterns of other cultures is even rarer than that on American friendships. From the sporadic treatments of the subject, it is difficult to compile a comprehensive account of friendship patterns in specific cultures. The following descriptions thus represent only the attempt to illuminate the characteristics of close interpersonal relationships in three countries selected to provide a sample of divergent friendship characteristics. (The case studies detailed later in this book focus on informants from these countries.)

Germany

When discussing Germany, one is first confronted with a political definition problem. A look at maps of "Germany" over the course of the centuries shows an incredible fluctuation in size and content (Barraclough, 1982). What started out as an assembly of Bavarian, Frankish, Saxon, and Swabian tribes and not so long ago was a mosaic of at times minute bishoprics, counties, duchies, electorates, landgraviates, margraviates, and principalities, just recently began forming more concise national boundaries. The unification of the East and West Germany left from the Second World War constitutes the latest culmination of this process. This political unit, however, (similar to many other countries) cannot hide the cultural diversity it contains. Thus, the old tribal structure still shines through, and Germany today consists of numerous smaller entities clearly differentiated by their cultures, dialects, and even the physiques and personalities of the constituents. Common generalizations, for example, about the thrifty Swabians, the carefree and easygoing Rhinelanders, the socially reserved North Germans, and the friendly and outgoing but often coarse Bavarians, are visible evidence of this diversity (Rectanus, Humphreys & Spence, 1984, p. 3; Shirer, 1981, p. 62). However, even though these differences exist and might actually in part influence friendship styles, they are--probably due to a lack of research--rarely mentioned in the respective literature. Most publications present their findings under the assumption of a national character and will be depicted thus here.

One of the most interesting comparisons between American and German interpersonal patterns was written by Lewin (1948). Despite its distant publication date, the findings of the treatise continue to reverberate in more recent literature and therefore serve well as a basis for the analysis. At the core of Lewin's comparison is a juxtaposition of American and German personality types. While persons from both cultures have the same number of personality layers, ranging centripetally from peripheral layers on the outside to an innermost center (Lewin lists five layers altogether), the layers that are considered public versus private domain are different in the two cultures. Thus, in the United States, all but the central fifth layer are public domain whereas in Germany only the outermost first layer is considered such.

This dichotomy results in several phenomena. The most obvious one concerns perceived social distance. The larger number of public layers in the United States by necessity contains a greater variety of contact features in a graded but fluid mixture of formal and informal functions. Americans therefore appear open and friendly, easily start conversations with strangers and invite people for lunch or into their homes quite readily. Social distance in Germany is much larger than in the United States, and the one peripheral public layer is characterized by formality and reserved solely for all external interactions, such as business relations and other impersonal events; humor, for example does not belong in the workplace in Germany (Kalberg, 1987, p. 609). For this reason Germans seem unfriendly (Tjioe, 1972, p. 151) or arrogant and formal (Kalberg, 1987, p. 610) to Americans who expect much greater congeniality in public situations and no obstacles to more amicable exchanges at such a peripheral point. This boundary between the thin public layer and the underlying private layer has to be penetrated to gain access to the friendliness and openness so unobstructed in the American pattern. But once this is achieved, one has already reached the private core of the German personality and a vast area of friendship potential with a gradual and now unrestricted transition from friendliness to warmth, compassion and finally to the most intimate regions. In other words, Germans see the private sphere as a refuge from all formal relationships (Kalberg, 1987, p. 610) and are protective of that refuge, but once inside, one has attained a level of closeness that can easily be expanded and is in fact expected to grow. Thus, the cultivation of friendships and their permanence is much more highly evaluated in Germany than in the United States (Kalberg, 1987, p. 612). The public and private layer situation for Americans is reversed. Whereas Americans are easily accessible in the outer layers (which is the fact often falsely interpreted as a promise of friendship by Germans and other foreigners), the innermost private core is very difficult to enter and is considered even less permeable than in Germans (Lewin, 1948, p. 23). Thus, Americans have relatively more close relations without a deep level of involvement and often less permanence (Lewin, 1948, pp. 24-25).

The image of public and private personality layers illuminates a number of related facets. On a minor scale, it is at least one reason why the accessible, public Americans prefer to leave their doors (in office and home) open, but Germans keep them shut (Lewin, 1948, p. 19). The model is also congruent with a ceremony that adds an element of formalization to German friendship which American friendships do not possess. This ceremony is called *Brüderschafttrinken* and requires that two people, each holding a glass of beer or wine, entwine arms, thus drink from their glasses, and possibly kiss each other on the cheeks or mouth (Rubin, 1985, p. 4). This ceremony precedes the change from the formal form of address, *Sie,* to the familiar *Du* and thus helps cross the threshold from the public to the private sphere.

On a larger scale, Lewin's analysis provides an explanation why Germans and other foreigners often judge American friendships as shallow or superficial. Assuming that many sojourners in the United States are mainly exposed to the public layers of Americans and never "crack the nut" of the intimate inner layer, it is indeed understandable why they would perceive an absence of depth. On the other hand, one can also comprehend why some Americans abroad value the relatively more easily attainable deeper emotional bonds inherent in German and other European friendship patterns, and why some feel that this closer involvement brings out hidden aspects of their personality (Winter, 1986, p. 316).

Another effect of the public and private layer dichotomy between Americans and Germans is the degree of compartmentalization. With Americans having to their avail so many public layers and thus a broad field of action for a variety of relationships, different areas of life are clearly separated (Lewin, 1948, p. 31) and relationships are often based on interests (Kalberg, 1987, p. 612). A case in point for this compartmentalization is the structure of American social events. When socializing in groups, Americans tend to have more or less brief contacts with many people, inquiring about occupations and interests at the beginning of conversations, and preferring more issue than person-oriented formats for these brief interactions (Kalberg, 1987, pp. 612-614). This is often said to be a sign for pragmatism and the search for mutual profitability (Winter, 1986, p. 316). By contrast, Germans approach relationships more holistically, trying to base friendships more on character than interests and preferring a slower pace and a longer observation period in the development of these friendships. Likewise, they frequently are frustrated by the hurried pace of American social gatherings and by being so quickly labeled according to their occupation or interests (Kalberg, 1987, pp. 612-614).

The more holistic orientation of Germans is deeply connected with another phenomenon. Whereas the outer personality layers are the seat of action and appearance, as is emphasized in the active, achievement-oriented American, the inner layers are the realm of morals and ideas (Lewin, 1948, p. 25). It is this inner focus combined with the more holistic perception that results in the great importance of ideology and related status in Germany and the fact that Germans tend to apply the whole person when confronted with a task (Lewin, 1948, pp. 25, 32). Therefore, whereas Americans are able to stay uninvolved and are also less in danger of personal friction because the sensitive inner layer of intimacy is small and closed, Germans seem more intense or even impatient, egotistical, and aggressive (Lewin, 1948, pp. 14, 25, 32; Tjioe, 1972, p. 151). If, for example, two politicians fight in the United States, they might emerge on cordial terms afterwards since the fight takes place in the safe, outer layers and can be compartmentalized there. In Germany, on the other hand, disagreement concerning politics or, in fact, any subject that matters involves the whole person, is, therefore, inseparable from moral disapproval and within friendships is often regarded as a tragedy (Lewin, 1948, p. 13; Mead, 1966, p. 40).

Because of the holistic orientation, Germans individually tend to be consistent and predictable, exhibiting the same persona even in different roles in life (Lewin, 1948, p. 31). And because the private layers of personality contain so much of human nature, groupings in Germany not only appear less homogenous than those in the United States (see, for example, the number and nature of political parties) (Lewin, 1948, pp. 26-29), but also have stronger insider/outsider boundaries so that group membership is not attained quickly but has to be earned (Kalberg, 1987, p. 606). In Germany, status is often a vehicle for group acceptance, rather than an agreeable or flamboyant personality as in the United States. At times, this difference leads to misunderstandings since a German in the United States might wait for acceptance because of status, but the American instead views the German as being unable to initiate in relationships (Kalberg, 1987, p. 608). Another related feature is that when a relationship *is* established or group membership achieved,

Americans in line with the abovementioned easygoing, uninvolved disposition do not give extreme weight to rights or duties; Germans, however, attach a sense of obligation to relationships and groups, at times compelling them to perform sacrifices or put personal interests in the background (Winter, 1986, p. 316).

In reviewing the last paragraph, the reader might perceive a seeming paradox between the homogeneity of American groups and the proverbial individualism of Americans. Hofstede (1986, p. 309), for example, groups Americans much higher on the individualism scale than Germans. This paradox might be resolved, if individualism is defined in contrast to collectivism in which persons belong to one or more in-groups with members protecting each other and expecting loyalty; thus individualsm is not so much marked by heterogeneity but by the fact that persons look after their own interests with low obligations in a loosely integrated society (Hofstede, 1986, p. 307). From a slightly different angle, the paradox between American individualism and membership in homogenous groups can also be explained by the fact that the act of joining groups and organizations in itself is an act of choice expressed by the individual (Paige, 1991, p. 49).

Besides the aforementioned characteristics of Germans in relation with their friendship patterns, research literature lists a few other factors that might be of importance. Thus, Germany is said to feature more clearly separated sex roles than the United States and much stronger uncertainty avoidance (Hofstede, 1986, p. 310), leading to a myriad of rules and behavior norms (Tjioe, 1972, p. 151).

Certainly more differences can be found between the American and German national characters which would stray, however, from the friendship focus at hand. But even with only the above findings in this specialized pool of information, it can be seen that the friendship patterns and interaction techniques of Americans and Germans vary significantly and that the cultural differences are generally underestimated (Winter, 1986, p. 332).

In conclusion, one word of caution needs to be reiterated. The above findings are generalizations and assume the existence of a national character on the American and German side. While predominant traits might exist, we need to keep in mind that there are individual differences, gender-specific practices (especially descriptions of

American friendship styles seem too often patterned according to male, independent idiosyncracies), and regional variations. Unfortunately, research in these areas is so minimal that it does not provide a sufficient basis for a more comprehensive analysis.

India

India, to a much greater extent than Germany, features an incredible diversity among its population. Not only are there predictable regional divisions with differences in history, geography, and customs, there are also about 20 major languages, a myriad of minor languages and distinctive dialects, racial discrepancies, and at times even functional tribal systems (e.g., Chatterjee, 1983, p. 199; Srivastava, 1960; Tyler, 1973, pp. 13, 16). Being the birthplace of Hinduism, Jainism, Sikhism, and Buddhism and also housing a sizeable minority of Muslims, Christians, Zoroastrians, and animists (Brigham Young University, 1993b, p. 2; Chatterjee, 1983b, p. 199), customs and behavior patterns associated with these religious faiths multiply the variety.

In addition, the old caste system still influences modern life. Originally a nonhereditary, occupation-based means for social hierarchization, castes became hereditary and a fairly unescapable determinant of one's role and status in society (Lannoy, 1971, pp. 137-167). The four primary castes of Brahmans (spiritual leaders and teachers), Kshatryas (government officals and military), Vaishyas (farmers and merchants), Sudras (helpers and servants), and the later added caste of the untouchables (menial laborers) were subdivided in a myriad of subcastes, each with major and minor differences in values, personality types, appropriate bahavior, customs, and lifestyles, and each with strong internal ties for sociability and security (Bishop, 1971, pp. 10-11; Lannoy, 1971, pp. 110, 138; Tyler, 1973, p. 5). With time, the caste system became a means of solidifying inequalities   and humiliations and allowed a heartless exploitation of the lower castes by the upper castes (Chatterjee, 1983, p. 202). But even though castes lost their quasi-legal status with the promulgation of the Indian Constitution in 1950, the structural system still exerts its power and especially in rural areas continues to determine or at least influence a person's functions, status, job opportunities, social handicaps, and lifestyle (Lannoy, 1971, pp. 247-248). With this much diversity and, needless to say, the absence of comprehensive literature concerning variations in general and friendship-related differences in specific, it is dangerous to generalize about anything in India. Yet, researchers purport that there are some pan-Indian traits that lend themselves to intercultural comparisons (Lannoy, 1971, p. 166; Tyler, 1973, p. 5).

At the base of these common features are in all likelihood some pervasive religious ideals that have become universal by their long history of contact and the importance of outstanding spiritual leaders like Gandhi (Brigham Young University, 1993b, p. 2). Thus, aspiring to freedom from possessions, simple living, spiritual development (Singh, 1962, pp. 124, 126), and a union with God that has as its goal not the eradication of personality but that of the ego and its egoistic pursuits, prizing individuals who illuminate the world (Brown, 1986, pp. 2, 23), are virtues that have left their mark on the broader value system of Indian life. When listing these values, researchers invariably include lack of covetousness, self-restraint, social harmony, absence of malice and hatred, benevolence, compassion, straightforwardness, and obedience (Bishop, 1971, p. 13; Brigham Young University, 1993b, p.2; Brown, 1986, p. 2; Sasaki, 1972, p. 17; Singh, Huang, & Thompson, 1962, pp. 124-131).

Some interculturally interesting phenomena are born out of this conglomeration. The ideals of freedom from covetousness and self-restraint, for example, are diametrically opposed to the widespread American goals of material wealth, success, power, and prestige (Singh, Huang, & Thompson, 1962, p. 126). Emotional self-restraint also precludes public touching and kissing, which is shunned in India (Singh, Huang, & Thompson, 1962, p. 124) and might be the reason for the adherence to established roles even in dissimilar life situations (Brown, R. H., 1986, pp. 14-15). The values of striving for social harmony and absence of malice and hatred, which might lead an Indian to agree in a divergence of opinions rather than upsetting the other person (Brigham Young University, 1993b, p. 2), has resulted in American interpretations of Indians as nonassertive and noncompetitive (Roland, 1986, p. 49). A related matter is the routine, even if incorrect, use of affirmatives, because saying no is considered impolite. Such a stance can lead to ambiguity considering promises and commitments (Chatterjee, 1983, p. 200). An interesting difference between Americans and Indians related to the values of benevolence and compassion was found by Miller, Bersoff, & Harwood (1990, pp. 34-45) in a study about helping behavior. Thus, when confronted with a series of cases in which others needed help, ranging from minor needs (e.g., asking for directions) to major life-threatening situations, Indians generally viewed responsiveness as an objective obligation whereas Americans saw helping others in moral terms only in serious cases.

The findings point to another difference between American and Indian value orientations, which will be discussed later in this section, namely the dichotomy between the American ideal of individual rights, autonomy, and freedom of choice and the Indian preference for a moral code giving priority to social duties and responsibilities. Research literature reports that the value of straightforwardness at times effects intercultural conflict in inquiries about someone's health as part of greetings. Whereas Americans tend to regard these inquiries as formulaic and usually answer the question *How are You?* with *I'm fine* or a variation thereof, Indians consider such an exchange superficial and a strain, preferring instead an honest account and viewing the resulting encounter as a shared experience with a possible therapeutic outcome (Brown, 1986, p. 13; Roland, 1986, p. 47). The last of the most frequently mentioned Indian values, obedience, also leads to predictable intercultural differences in that Indians are more authoritarian than Americans, exhibit automatic responses to power and authority often at the expense of their individuality, ambition, or creativity, and seem too resigned to the hierarchical setting prevalent in India (Brown, 1986, p. 4; Chatterjee, 1983, p. 205; Singh, Huang, & Thompson, 1962, p. 126; Tyler, 1973, p. 4). Again, the dichotomy between individuality and conformity is at the core of the dispute and brings up the subject of the family, which is most comprehensively discussed in the relationship-oriented literature about India.

Families, in India, are the basic and most tightly knit unit in a society where group membership (beyond families, to subcastes and castes) is of immense importance and not only a source of protection, comfort, and support but also a means of identity formation (Brigham Young University, 1993b, p. 3; Brown, 1986, p. 18; Coelho, 1986, p. 184).

Thus, the Indian's self-image is defined by the family and community to the point where unique aspects of individuals are disregarded, people forfeit their own boundaries when immersed in the family, lose initiative and the incentive for personal effort, and become helpless and dependent on the power of the group and at times prone or least exposed to parasitism (Brigham Young University, 1993b, p. 3; Brown, 1986, p. 8; Chatterjee, 1983, p. 205; Coelho, 1986, p. 184; Lannoy, 1971, pp. 89, 112). Needless to say, the family bond also brings with it an extensive set of obligations and ritual duties, remaining a haven of support but also retaining its firm hold throughout a person's life (Brown, 1986, pp. 3-8; Coelho, 1986, p. 184).

It is understandable that many Indian students, suddenly deprived of this primary network of support, feel insecure, self-conscious, and lonely when entering the United States (Klein, Alexander, Miller, Haack, & Bushnell, 1986, p. 120). In contrast to India, a person in the United States is often defined by rebellion against the family and sets out to become independent, task-oriented, and autonomous, pursuing a flexible, many-sided life with much self-indulgence, and assigning a secondary role to the original family in adulthood (Brown, 1986, pp. 4-9; Singh, Huang, & Thompson, 1962, p. 131). Even though the American need for privacy and desire to lead one's own life is foreign to the Indian worldview, might cause feelings of discomfort, and frequently ensues in complaints about the indifferent, busy, and self-centered American (Klein, Alexander, Miller, Haack, & Bushnell, 1986, p. 120; Roland, 1986, p. 45; Singh, Huang, & Thompson, 1962, pp. 128-131), Indian sojourners usually adapt quickly to this and other different social arrangements (Roland, 1986, p. 48). This adaptability is a direct result of the family structure in India. When Indians grow up, they are continuously surrounded by other people (Brown, 1986, p. 13; Tyler, 1973, p. 2). The complete lack of privacy fosters social competence and sensitivity, an enjoyment of social life and concern for other people, and a desire to dedicate one's energy to relationships instead of other pursuits (Brown, 1986, pp. 12-13; Roland, 1986, p. 48; Singh, Huang, & Thompson, 1962, p. 131).

It has also been stated, however, that Indian social confidence and interpersonal warmth at times only extends along familiar group lines, and that uncertainty and distrustfulness mark some relationships outside of kinship or group bonds (Lannoy, 1971, p. 112; Tyler, 1973, p. 6). This phenomenon is attributed to the fact that children grow up in extended and surrogate families with not one or two but a myriad of reference persons and an often elusive father. The ensuing feelings of uncertainty and ambivalence about the love relations of the family are exacerbated when relationships are voluntary and based only on respect and affection (Lannoy, 1971, p. 112). The diversity of role models in the typical Indian family structure has yet another side effect. Since there is no single well-defined model, it is difficult for a child to develop a respective personality. Thus, Indians frequently seem to have multiple personalities with autonomously functioning unrelated traits (Lannoy, 1971, p. 88), at times causing Westerners to see Indians as deceitful, insincere, and incapable of holding on to a unified one-dimensional reality. Whereas this verdict is a negative interpretation of a facet of Indian personality tendencies, from a different perspective one might say that the seemingly missing positive traits exist, albeit fleetingly, and that the phenomenon adds a pleasant versatility and present-orientedness to the Indian character (Tyler, 1973, p. 6). It also has to be noted that the Indian thinking style, in contrast to the American linear thought process, is spiral and nonlinear. An uninitiated observer might falsely attribute this nonlinearity to the lack of dependability and straightforwardness, thus further adding to the unfavorable impression (Lannoy, 1971, p. 423).

The subject matter of friendship is closely related to family concerns in India, not only because friendships are often mediated by family ties (Brown, 1986, p. 12), but also because many social patterns learned in the ever important family translate into nonkinship relations. Thus, the value placed on relationships instead of individualistic pursuits of autonomy and success shows in a high degree of affiliation, nurturance, mutual help, sensitivity, love, and intimacy (Roland, 1986, p. 44; Singh, Huang, & Thompson, 1962, pp. 126-130). Friendships are focused on an affinity of hearts, not interests, and are considered permanent (Brown, 1986, pp. 10-14), carrying with them obligations and responsibilities (Miller, Bersoff, & Harwood, 1990, pp. 34, 45). The relative paucity of these traits in the generalized American friendship pattern leads Brown (1986, p. 14) to describe an American's life as a "grand tour of handshakes" or a "hall into which people step for a minute on their way somewhere else" and compare its relationship aspects in theatrical terms with "a mass of bits performed by half-known actors." An Indian, by contrast, once he or she has found a nourishing relationship, "wants to grow a garden around it," and "each relationship thus becomes a play with many scenes" in an atmosphere of "unmovable permanence."

Another major difference between American and Indian friendship patterns is that the above characterization of Indian friendships holds true across genders, for women *and* men. Even though women and men are traditionally more separated than in the United States and are not allowed to intermingle as much (Lannoy, 1971, pp. 128-129), differences in love, self-disclosure, activities, and the functions of friendship between each sex as a whole were only found in the United States, not in India (Berman, Murphy-Berman, & Pachauri, 1988, p. 69). Thus, Indian men are as free as women to form intimate friendships with revelation of deep feelings, failures, and worries and to show their affection physically by holding hands, for example (Brown, 1986, pp. 10-11; Berman, Murphy-Berman, & Pachauri, 1988, p. 68; Roland, 1986, p. 44). Berman, Murphy-Berman, & Pachauri (1988, pp. 69-70) comment on the phenomenon:

> At first this seems surprising. One thinks of the United States as a "liberated," androgenous society in which roles for males and females are increasingly merging and becoming less and less distinct. On the other hand, one thinks of India as a place where sex roles are very traditional and highly differentiated. The answer to this puzzle may be found . . . in the role that males are allowed to play in each society. Because Indian males are allowed a full gamut of emotional expression, they can provide all functions and activities of friendship to each other, unlike their U.S. counterparts who cannot provide some of the functions (e.g., problem sharing) or engage in some of the activities (e.g., private conversations).

Whether concerning friendship patterns in general or gender differences in specific, the discrepancies between the two cultures emerge in common complaints of Indian students in the United States. Thus, Indian sojourners often comment that friendships are centered around academic matters, their role as cultural ambassador, or activities, such as sports (Klein, Alexander, Miller, Haack, & Bushnell, 1986, pp. 118-126). While this arrangement might be satisfactory for some, others find the inherent lack of intimacy painful and complain that even after years, relationships remain superficial and devoid of comfort (Klein, Alexander, Miller, Haack, & Bushnell, 1986, p. 115; Roland, 1986, p. 45). Besides this lack of closeness, ethnocentrism is mentioned as a barrier to deep friendship, and students are often pained about American ignorance and indifference concerning social and cultural conditions in India (Klein, Alexander, Miller, Haack, & Bushnell, 1986, pp. 120, 126).

Again, one has to keep in mind that a good part of comparative intercultural literature deals with generalizations and that in the United States and maybe even more so in India the diversity of the populace and changing conditions have to be considered. Thus, straying from all the abovementioned, middleground generalizations, on one extreme end of the spectrum, we are confronted with tribal practices still in existence in modern India. Some of the tribes, for example, feature institutionalized friendships with inaugural rituals, lifelong obligations (e.g., shared rites of passage duties and expenses), and an importance equal to or even surpassing kinship relations (Srivastava, 1960). On the other end of the spectrum, one has to keep in mind that Western beliefs of individual freedom, social justice, and universal education have begun to leave their mark on India (Bishop, 1971, p. 15), expanding the cultural repertoire and changing some traditional patterns and customs. Generalizations do not include extremes and changes, and for this and other reasons have to be treated with the necessary caution.

Taiwan

Taiwan, or the Republic of China, came into existence in 1949 when the Nationalist Chinese government was expelled from mainland China (the People's Republic of China) by the Communists, repaired to the island of Formosa, and took with it a large number of middle class Chinese (Chang, 1973, p. 67; Stover & Stover, 1976, p. 80). Taiwan's population now is mostly Chinese with only a small minority of Taiwanese aborigines; the official dialect is Mandarin Chinese (Brigham Young University, 1993c, p. 2).

Considering the vast geographical variation within mainland China, one might also assume a great amount of cultural variation. However, even though researchers do admit to some differences between the culturally and linguistically homogenous North (generally Mandarin in language) and the ethnically and linguistically diverse South (Hoosain, 1986, p. 48; Stover & Stover, 1976, pp. 104-105), basic values, socialization patterns, and personality traits are said to have been uniform and unaltered for generations (e.g., Hoosain, 1986, p. 47; Yang, K. S., 1986, pp. 107-111). When adding Taiwan to the picture, two interesting facets emerge. One is that in 1949, Chinese from almost every major province came to Taiwan, resulting in a fairly representative sample of the overall Chinese population (Yang, K. S., 1986, p. 107). Thus, research literature purports, in most respects China and Taiwan still share the same culture (Hoosain, 1986, pp. 47-48; Kao, 1987; Yang, K. S., 1986 , p. 111). On the other hand, even though it is a political crime in both China and Taiwan to suggest that Taiwan is separate from the mainland (Butterfield, 1982, p. 57), it can be argued that the two populaces have been physically kept apart long enough to result in some cultural differences. And indeed, recent research has shown that modernizations in Taiwan (closely linked to the transformation from an agricultural to an industrial society) have also brought about cultural changes, in general of a Westernizing nature (Ho, 1986, p. 36; Liu, 1986, p. 104; Yang, K. S., 1986). Thus, Taiwan is said to exhibit an increasing individualistic orientation, leading to more democratic attitudes, autonomy, critical thinking, extroversion, competition, and self-indulgence and to less authoritarian attitudes, nurturance, endurance, social restraint, self-control, and harmoniousness (Ho, 1986, p. 36; Liu, 1986, p. 105; Yang, K. S., 1986, pp. 161-162). These changes, however, are in their beginning stages and are as of yet merely starting to outline themselves. Old traditions are still prevalent and will, thus, be the focus of the description below.

In most dicussions of Chinese culture, reference is made to the ecological and philosophical or religious base for the development of general patterns and national characteristics. From an ecological view, it is pointed out that the physical features of the land were conducive to the establishment of an agricultural subsistence economy which, together with the social division between peasantry and land-owning gentry, produced a hierarchical, collectivistic social system marked by structural tightness, general familiazation, and social homogeneity (Yang, K. S., 1986, p. 162). What created and kept the system in place was partly the fact that the single-landscape economy could only support a finite number of landlords who, due to the scarcity of resources, could keep tenants and even day laborers dependent and subordinated by making work a favor and competitive (Stover & Stover, 1976, pp. 110-111). Maintaining the status quo was also aided by widespread Taoist beliefs that enlightenment and fulfillment will come through lack of ambition and an empty mind (Stover & Stover, 1976, p. 52). Thus, uneducated peasants continued toiling from a position of political apathy and supplication, and landlords continued collecting rent without even the effort of supervision (Stover & Stover, 1976, p. 111). Hand in hand with ecological considerations, but maybe even more influential, was the dominant philosophical or religious doctrine of Confucianism. The brainchild of Chung-ni K'ung or Confucius, who lived in the 5th century B.C., Confucianism postulates that (a) humans exist through and are defined by their relationships to others, (b) these relationships are hierarchical, and (c) social order is ensured by everybody honoring their role requirements (Bond & Hwang, 1986, pp. 214-216). These three suppositions concerning relationships, hierarchy, and role requirements have had a far-reaching effect on Chinese culture.

Thus, the postulate that humans exist through and are defined by their relationships is the core principle of the collectivism prevalent in China. In contrast to loosely integrated individualistic societies like the United States, which are marked by self-orientation, individual identities, independence, high privacy needs, self-indulgence, verbal communication with explicit meanings, and activeness (Hofstede, 1986, p. 307; Hoosain, 1986, p. 53; Ting-Toomey, 1989, pp. 357-368; Yang, K. S., 1986, p. 120), collectivistic societies are structurally tight and evolve around groups and their smooth functioning (Hofstede, 1986, p. 307).

Thus, Chinese typically belong to two or more in-goups which protect their members in exchange for loyalty (Hofstede, 1986, p. 307; Kapp, 1983, p. 11). This loyalty requires that group members help the group, achieve with a social orientation, support each other, and immerse themselves in mutual dependence (Redding & Wang, 1986, p. 272;

Singh, Huang, & Thompson, 1962, p. 125; Yang, K. S., 1986, pp. 114, 122). Independent action and self-centeredness are socially disapproved; instead people willingly conform to and gain their worth and position from the group (Hoosain, 1986, p. 122; Kuo & Spees, 1983, p. 115; Singh, Huang, & Thompson, 1962, p. 128; Yang, K. S., 1986, p. 122). Members of collectivistic societies derive satisfaction from social life and the concern for others, and are usually described as being warm, sympathetic, benevolent, and good-natured, at least in relation to fellow in-group members (Bond & Hwang, 1986, p. 234; Kuo & Spees, 1983, p. 115; Yang, K. S., 1986). Based on the need for the equal distribution of the limited resources and in the ensuing Confucian precept to curtail individual desires, great weight is put on maintaining harmonious relationships and interpersonal equilibrium. This in turn necessitates self-control and social restraint to the point where open disagreements are side-stepped and the expression of emotions in general is inhibited (which is especially true for women, with the ideal being one of taciturn, shy, and passive females) (Alter, Klopf, & Cambra, 1980, p. 12; Bond & Hwang, 1986; Tjioe, 1972, p. 219; Yang, K. S., 1986). Thus, Chinese appear cautious, patient, socially introverted, practical, and less impulsive, spontaneous, and excitable than their individualistic American counterparts (Yang, K. S., 1986). In addition, Chinese show a lower level of aggression, the absence of which is nurtured from early on by punishing aggressive behavior in children. Related to this phenomenon, Chinese also exhibit a lower need for dominance and leadership (Tjioe, 1972, p. 221; Yang, K. S., 1986, pp. 111, 122). Western interpretations of this overall disposition at times lead to stereotyping the Chinese as obsequious and weak-willed (Bond & Hwang, 1986, p. 218). As with any trait, however, we can choose to see the positive or negative side. Thus, from a Chinese perspective, the collectivistic mindset propagates prudence in not disrupting present relationships and brings with it a security in interpersonal matters, surety in direction, and ease in decision-making missing in individualistic societies (Bond & Hwang, 1986, p. 218; Liu, 1986, p. 105).

When comparing Chinese with U.S. society, some side effects of collectivism deserve mention. Thus, the avoidance of disharmony leads to an indirect and ambiguous mode of communication much opposed to the more direct and straightforward style of Americans (Kapp, 1983, p.

20; Paige, 1991, p. 50). According to the Western theory of sincerity, "the authentic self does not wear a false face" (Stover & Stover, 1976, p. 202), and because of their indirectness (and, for example, their reluctance to say *no* directly), the Chinese are often described as hiding behind formal niceties and are consequently being stereotyped as inscrutable, deceitful, and insincere (Stover & Stover, 1976, pp. 202, 205). However, according to Chinese standards, not introducing friction into the smooth working of relationships and saving the feelings of others takes priority over direct self-expression, at least as far as in-group relations are concerned; strangers at times are not considered intimate enough for the courtesy of a lie and may, therefore, be treated rudely (Stover & Stover, 1976, p. 203). Chinese often regard their sophisticated awareness of the difference between form and content and their world of complex, subtle, and enduring relationships as superior, and may consider Westeners ignorant for not appreciating the intricate over the direct and simple (Stover & Stover, 1976, pp. 203-206).

Another side effect of the collectivistic mode of thinking concerns the need for affiliation. Due to well-defined and pervasive group memberships, inclusion needs seem to be satisfied. Consequently, Chinese test low on affiliativeness in contrast to Americans whose concern with social success and peer acceptance leads to a relatively high need for affiliation, sociability, and gregariousness (Alter, Klopf, & Cambra, 1980, pp. 7-8, 12; Bond & Hwang, 1986, p. 257; Yang, K. S., 1986, pp. 113, 122). That this need for affiliation in American society is often filled with numerous but fleeting relationships is explained by Cohen (1961a, pp. 314-317; 1961b, pp. 275, 382) who correlates society structures with friendship patterns. Thus, the societal system of the maximally solidary community (with definite social or physical boundaries between social groupings) is correlated with inalienable friendships; the solidary-fissile community (still with definite boundaries but with looser kindship ties which are not solidified into corporate, land-owning goups) is matched with close friendships in which mutual assistance is given freely in times of need; the nonnucleated society (with isolated families) is marked by more casual friendships of narrowed and reluctant sharing; and the individuated social structure (with individuated accumulation of wealth as an end in itself) predominantly features expedient friendships whose functions are temporary and mostly instrumental. This categorization also highlights why the Chinese, coming from solidary-fissile to maximally solidary communities, expect support and protection; whereas the nonnucleated to individuated Americans at times even resent it (Kapp, 1983, p. 11).

The second postulate of Confucianism, establishing hierarchical relationships, also has far-reaching implications in Chinese society. Originating from a desire to establish loyalty to the sovereign and eliminate competition for the throne (Stover & Stover, 1976, pp. 50, 150), a system of stratification was created in China that required submission to authority and unquestionable obedience, resulting in a belief of external control and the importance of social order (Bond & Hwang, 1986, p. 213; Ho, 1986, pp. 35-36; Singh, Huang, & Thompson, 1962, p. 126; Yang, K. S., 1986, p. 126). Thus, unless a Chinese clearly knows that he or she is the authority in a role relationship, "the best policy is always to behave like a subordinate and to treat the other as an authority" (Yang, K. S., 1986, p. 128). Since Americans have an internal seat of control, embracing autonomy and assertiveness, this philosophy has led to the perception of Chinese as passive in interactions, inhibited, self-abasing, and easily taken advantage of (Tjioe, 1972, pp. 53, 118; Yang, K. S., 1986). However stereotypical this verdict may be, research literature does agree on some undesirable side effects of strict authoritarianism. Thus, it is said to generate a rigidity in personality, stifle creativity, produce a lack of cognitive complexity, inhibit verbal and ideational flow, and lead to a perceived incapacity to influence events (Ho, 1986, p. 36; Hoosain, 1986, pp. 53-54; Liu, 1986, p. 103; Yang, K. S., 1986, p. 126). If these negative consequences can be minimized with a more moderate authoritarianism, as it is gaining acceptance in present-day Taiwan, its positive effects of emotional stability of the individual and stability of family and society, however, may increase its attractiveness even in American eyes (Liu, 1986, p. 104).

The third Confucian postulate, of honoring role requirements, is integrally tied to the hierarchical society structure, leading to considerations of proper conduct in interpersonal relationships; i.e., correct behavior according to one's position in the hierarchy, and external expectations and social norms rather than internal wishes (Bond & Hwang, 1986, p. 243; Ho, 1986, pp. 35-36; Yang, K. S., 1986, pp.

129, 161). Resembling a "carefully calculated science" (Butterfield, 1982, p. 48), the rules for proper conduct are a complex maze of relationship categories, sets of social rights and responsibilities, and strategies for face protection and harmony maintenance. Bond & Hwang (1986, p. 215) mention five cardinal relationship categories of paramount importance in Chinese society: sovereign/subject, father/son, elder brother/younger brother, husband/wife, and friend/friend; Stover & Stover (1976, p. 203) add two more in elder/junior and host/guest. It has to be pointed out that these and all other relationships are unequal, and that age difference creates an automatic hierarchy (even between friends) with a wide range of prerogatives and authority concerning the senior versus junior member (Bond & Hwang, 1986, p. 215; Stover & Stover, 1976, pp. 203-204).

Superimposed on the categories of relationships are three modes of interaction or degrees of closeness. Bond & Hwang (1986, pp. 223-224) call them *expressive ties* (between family members), *instrumental ties* (temporary and anomymous for the attainment of goals; e.g., between customer and salesperson), and *mixed ties* (between members of a network which includes an expressive element but is based on favors and their reciprocation). The fixed power relationships or connections of the mixed tie mode are also called *guanxi* (Butterfield, 1982, p. 44). *Guanxi* are cultivated by Chinese if the previously mentioned cardinal relationships are not sufficient to provide the services and goods needed. They are different from friendships in that they are not based on compatibility but on expected material benefits (Stover & Stover, 1976, p. 207). Chinese are well-aware with whom they have *guanxi* and what moral obligations are involved (Butterfield, 1982, p. 44; Yang, M. M. H., 1986). For Westerners it is at times difficult to determine "just what mix of pragmatism and genuine affection make up relationships" (Turner-Gottschang & Reed, 1987, p. 55).

Closely connected with the cardinal relationship and the three modes of interaction is the concept of *face*. Face is the image of self in social intercourse and the desire to present oneself in terms of approved attributes (Bond & Hwang, 1986, p. 244). Thus, enhancing or saving face for oneself and one's group is important and manifests itself in behaviors such as showing off appreciated qualities, complimenting, and not denying favors directly (Bond & Hwang, 1986, pp. 246-247).

Mixed tie relations require putting forth one's best image and therefore necessitate a lot of face work. In line with the collectivistic lack of expressiveness and the preamble of not showing emotions in public, authentic behavior is only revealed in expressive ties (Bond & Hwang, 1986, p. 245; Stover & Stover, 1976, p. 202). Thus, the self-disclosing of deep feelings and assistance in life crises are mainly reserved for the family (Bond & Hwang, 1986, p. 250).

Traditionally motivated by necessity (due to the absence of other helping institutions), family unity is of utmost importance (Brigham Young University, 1993c, p. 2; Stover & Stover, 1976, p. 152). Being the smallest unit of society, the family represents a microcosm of Confucian thought summarized in the term *filial piety* (Stover & Stover, 1976, p. 150). Thus, collectivistic principles are fulfilled by family loyalty and mutual dependence (Bond & Hwang, 1986, p. 254; Hoosain, 1986, p. 50). A hierarchy is established, usually in favor of patrilinear considerations (Stover & Stover, 1976, pp. 153-154), and role requirements are followed by the glorification of father and mother, the submission of the children to the parents' wishes, the (sometimes oppressive) protection of women and young ones, and the overall adherence to the prescribed conduct (Bond & Hwang, 1986, p. 254; Stover & Stover, 1976, pp. 150, 157). Considering this importance of the family, it comes as no surprise that three out of five of Bond and Hwang's cardinal relationships are familial, leaving only sovereign/subject and friend/friend on the outside (Bond & Hwang, 1986, p. 215). Even though the family is so encompassing, being one of the cardinal relationships gives close friendships import. Thus, research literature agrees that Chinese friendship patterns are marked by nurturance, endurance, and mutual obligations, offering psychological as well as material rewards, and assurances and intimacies missing in many American friendships (Butterfield, 1982, pp. 47-48; Yang, K. S., 1986, p. 109). With this background of belonging and sharing, many Chinese students in the United States tend to feel inadequate and lonely, complain about shallow relationships and discrimination (Chang, 1973, p. 68; Kuo & Spees, 1983, p. 115), often finding support solely in familiar bonds with fellow Chinese students.

In conclusion to this section on Chinese culture and maybe culture characterizations in general, it has to be reiterated that the presented pictures are generalizations and illustrate traditional interaction patterns. As with all generalizations, the line separating them from negative stereotypes is very thin, and observers or analysts of another culture's behavior patterns often fall prey to ethnocentric temptations of regarding out-group conduct as psychopathic and inferior, and individuals of that culture exhibiting more acceptable behavior as mere exceptions to the rule (Bond & Hwang, 1986, p. 222; Gudykunst, 1991, pp. 87-88). It is of immense importance to keep an open mind, seeing both sides of the medal and realizing that the positive aspects we perceive in a culture are often integrally tied to or even direct side effects of the negatively perceived traits. When foreign students in the United States are asked to list the most desirable characteristics of Americans, for example, they frequently describe them as friendly, optimistic, active, frank, and innovative (Bond & Hwang, 1986, p. 237; Chang, 1973, p. 68; Kapp, 1983, p. 11). We should not forget, however, that these traits are simply the more attractive byproducts of the same individualistic mindset that causes the more negative attributes about which foreign students often complain. The situation is identical, of course, for other cultures. Caution is also in place concerning the permanence of national characteristics. In addition to frequently having ethnocentric overtones and not attending to individual differences, generalizations usually focus on traditional patterns and do not include recent developments. Cultures, however, are in flux more than ever, and it has to be seen, for example, how the changes in present-day Germany, India, and Taiwan will effect established cultural norms in the future.

Chapter 4

Intercultural Friendship Formation

Research literature agrees that foreign student satisfaction and well-being in the United States are integrally tied to host country interaction in general and the development of close friendships with Americans in specific (Locke, 1988; Rohrlich & Martin, 1991, p. 174; Searle & Ward, 1990, p. 458). Close host country contacts are also of immense importance in facilitating overall adjustment and are said to be the most influential factor in changing international images (Dziegielewska, 1988, p. 33; Furnham & Alibhai, 1985, p. 710; Yum, 1988, p. 775). Thus, the phenomenon of friendship satisfies all or most of the conditions usually posited for the reduction of stereotypes and ethnocentric attitudes in intergroup contact (i.e., cooperation, equal status and competence, value similarity, positive outcomes, future interaction, individuation of interactants, intimate rather than casual contact, voluntariness, variety of contexts, equal number of interactants, and favorable climate) (cited in Gudykunst, 1991, pp. 79-80; cited in Yum, 1988, p. 775). Yet, the reality of intercultural friendship on U.S. campuses often falls short of the ideal. Indeed, the red thread through all of the respective research literature is foreign student disappointment with the lack of American friends (e.g., Furnham & Alibhai, 1985, p. 719; Hull, 1978, p. 223) and the fact that, if friendships do exist, they are usually less intense than expected and center around academic matters and activities, rather than intimate personal concerns (Roland, 1986, p. 126). Especially during the first year of sojourns, contacts are limited beyond modest expectations, and students often feel insecure, self-conscious, lonely, and powerless (Owie, 1982, p. 182; Roland, 1986, pp. 120-121). This social alienation from the host country can have different effects: It can lead to physical isolation and a retreat into the private world; it can cause an immersion into work and studies; or it can foster a banding together with fellow nationals or students from other countries (Owie, 1982, p. 165; Roland, 1986, p. 121; Strom, 1988, p. 5; Winter, 1986, p. 334). Thus, Bochner, McLeod, and Lin (1977, p. 191) found that of the three social networks of foreign students the primary one is monocultural and functions as an outlet for ethnic and cultural values among conationals. It is followed by a secondary network with host nationals that serves mainly instrumental purposes, such as academic and professional assistance. The tertiary, much less salient network consists of other internationals and fulfills recreational needs. Whereas interaction with fellow nationals can alleviate some of the adjustment stress and consequently be of vital importance to sojourners (Bochner, McLeod, & Lin, 1977, p. 292), a prolonged and exclusive reliance on home country support can have distinct disadvantages. Thus, it has been shown that sojourn satisfaction increases, the more close friends are from the host country and the fewer close friends are from the home country (Locke, 1988). Some foreign students point out that fellow nationals are arbitrarily thrown together and that the pool of truly suitable friends is therefore limited; they also remark that conational friendships ensue in too many obligations (parties, help, etc.) and often focus on gossip about other people's sojourn experiences and degrees of undesirable assimilation (Tjioe, 1972, p. 124). In addition, foreign student isolation from host country interactions can create a vicious circle of impeded English improvement and perpetual contact difficulties (Bochner, Hutnik, & Furnham, 1985, p. 692).

Presupposing this mostly undesirable status quo and the absence of formal rules for establishing and maintaining intercultural friendships (Argyle & Henderson, 1984, p. 213), the question arises of what exactly influences intercultural friendship formation. Concerning the specific case of foreign students in the United States, 12 key factors can be identified: culture, personality, self-esteem, friendship elements, expectations, adjustment stage, cultural knowledge, communicative competence, external variables, proximity, U.S. elements, and what we may call chemistry (see Figure 1).

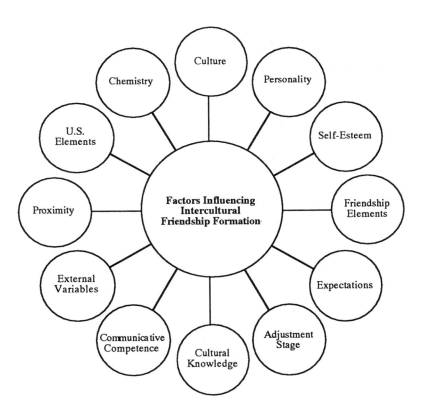

Figure 1. Factors influencing the formation of intercultural friendship.

The first five variables (culture, personality, self-esteem, friendship elements, and expectations) thereby focus on the predisposition of the individual sojourner. Adjustment stage, cultural knowledge, and communicative competence comprise the major factors present in the testing ground of the actual sojourn. External variables and proximity might be labeled auxiliary and add minor influences. Whereas the factors just listed are all to some extent influenceable and changeable by the sojourners, the last two (U.S. elements and chemistry) are givens and largely out of their control.

Culture

The first of the key factors is culture. Culture, of course, is a vast concept. Even if one can delineate cultural versus political boundaries and focuses on deep as opposed to formal components of culture, a myriad of aspects can be considered. They range from basic assumptions and value systems; the relationship between humans and nature; social structure; sex roles; sources of support; the importance of status; the locus of control; conflict resolution; mobility; the concepts of achievement, work, and play; uncertainty avoidance; past, present, and future orientation; and thought patterns; to verbal communication styles and nonverbal communication aspects (kinesics, proxemics, and haptics). Aspects of deep culture also include dichotomies such as individualism versus collectivism, doing versus being, the importance of objects versus interpersonal relationships, monochronic time versus polychronic time, and many more. Cultures can differ along all of these criteria and influence intercultural friendship formation even though some may play a more prominent role than others. Thus, invariably the distinction between individualistic and collectivistic outlooks is mentioned as a major variable in intercultural interaction. The dichotomy thereby often serves as an umbrella for a whole host of differences, including self- versus other-orientation, low versus high obligation, low versus high duration, high versus low spread, low versus high context (i.e., meaning explicit in message versus meaning embedded in setting or internalized) and verbal versus nonverbal communication prevalence. If two potential interactants are fairly typical representatives of individualistic and collectivistic cultures respectively, these differences have to be dealt with and can pose overwhelming obstacles in the development of the friendship.

Indeed, researchers have found that the dissimilarity of cultures in general, also called *social distance*, is a powerful predictor for difficulties in sociocultural adjustment (Du Bois, 1974, p. 78; Rohrlich & Martin, 1991, p. 164; Schaffer, 1966, p. 27; Searle & Ward, 1990, pp. 452, 457). Cultural similarity, on the other hand, gives attributional confidence; i.e., makes behavior explanations and predictions easier, and therefore increases interpersonal attraction during initial encounters, paving the way for deeper involvement (Lee & Boster, 1991, p. 191). Since one of the functions of close relationships is to affirm one's self and identity, it comes as no surprise that foreign students from cultures dissimilar to the host culture often band together with conationals or fellow students from similar or neighboring countries (Furnham & Alibhai, 1985, p. 721; Rubin, 1985, pp. 52-54). In the case of a foreign student from a collectivistic culture in the individualistic United States, this bonding is further aided by the automatic, preexisting group memberships and the frequent absence of peer support for venturing out and establishing relationships beyond the conational network (Paige, 1983, p. 109; Tjioe, 1972, p. 124). The fate of social isolation is sealed when unfavorable attitudes, prejudice, and discrimination against foreign-looking individuals on the part of the host country nationals create additional barriers and solidified intergroup relations (Schaffer, 1966, p. 24; Ting-Toomey, 1989, p. 359). Thus, on the extreme ends of the social distance continuum, culture dissimilarity contributes to social isolation, whereas culture similarity facilitates intercultural interaction.

As with all generalizations, we have to keep in mind, however, that there is variety among individuals and not everybody fits the typical mold. People from all cultures have the potential for unique interpersonal styles and in their individual identities might be closer to a given contact culture than others (Dziegielewska, 1988, p. 57; Roland, 1986, p. 119). Just as these personal perceptions of similarity ultimately determine social distance, care has to be taken that each person is seen as an individual and not labeled with national generalizations that do not apply (Dziegielewska, 1988, p. 199; Roland, 1986, p. 119).

Personality

Personality is the second key factor influencing friendship formation. Research literature agrees that personality is tied to culture at least in one major respect. Thus, individuals can define their identities along personal or cultural dimensions, leading to the identification of five different personality types (Ting-Toomey, 1986, p. 122). Balanced identifiers have clear personal and cultural identities; personal identifiers have a clear view of themselves but no strong cultural identity; cultural identifiers are less sure of their personal self but have a great understanding of themselves as cultural beings; marginal identifiers are low on both their personal and cultural scale; and ambivalent identifiers experience perpetual tension between personal and cultural identity (Ting-Toomey, 1986, pp. 122-125).

Strom (1988, pp. 191-197) found that people with a strong cultural identification--possibly out of a fear of losing their identities--spend their energies in the home-country milieu, do not interact as much with host nationals, and consequently have the least number of American friends. Being at least somewhat cultureless, personal and marginal identifiers have more friends and are better adjusted to the host society. Related to this phenomenon, it might be pointed out that individuals who do not define themselves along the lines of their mainstream home culture often find support in marginal groups of fellow outsiders (Rubin, 1985, pp. 52-54). These groups may have an ethnic or sexual-orientation focus, and in being semi-imposed by discriminatory practices in the mainstream culture, may exhibit an ambivalence between choice and self-doubt hidden behind defensiveness (Rubin, 1985, pp. 48, 52-54). However, they may also serve to provide a haven for people of certain political persuasions (e.g., environmentalists, socialists, neofascists), people with a certain common lifestyle (e.g., hippies, the ultra-rich of the international jet-set), intellectuals, artists, and similar groups marginal in their specific societies. These *global ingroups* cross borders and create a common ground for intercultural encounters, eclipsing other comparatively minor cultural dissimilarities.

Besides the nature of identification, other personality factors have been found to influence successful adjustment and intercultural interaction. Among them are empathy, patience, flexibility, broad categorization, resilience, resourcefulness, tolerance for ambiguity, world-mindedness, preparedness for change, extraversion, honesty, and sense of humor (Althen, 1988, pp. 150-151; Gudykunst, 1991, pp. 89, 117; Kim, Y. Y., 1989, p. 277; Kim, Y. Y., 1991, pp. 269-271; Paige, 1983, p. 110; Rohrlich & Martin, 1991, p. 164; Searle & Ward, 1990, p. 457). In general then, open and creative individuals with stable self-images and a high degree of sensitivity towards others possess a favorable starting position considering intercultural contact, whereas closed, rigid, and habitual personalities marked by a strong cultural definition and intergroup anxiety are at a disadvantage (Kim, Y. Y., 1991, pp. 269-271; Strom, 1988, p. 191; Winter, 1986, p. 327).

Self-Esteem

The third key factor concerning intercultural friendship formation, self-esteem, goes hand in hand with personality to the extent that one of its aspects, self-awareness, might be grouped in either category. Self-awareness and self-knowledge are the prerequisites of self-acceptance and therewith self-esteem. Taking it a step further, self-awareness, self-knowledge, and self-acceptance lead to other-awareness, other-knowledge, and other-acceptance and are, therefore, important ingredients in effective communication and successful intercultural contact (Saral, 1979, p. 79; Ting-Toomey, 1989, p. 361). If individuals know themselves, they are better able to disclose their identities and reduce uncertainty in interactions, which is an essential element in the development of close relationships (Ting-Toomey, 1986, pp. 118-120). Research has found that individuals with high self-esteem are less alienated from others and more open and direct in their need for affiliation and friendship (cited in Strom, 1988, p. 195). People with self-confidence, and joy and pride in their ability to function in the new environment are also more likely to reach out, initiate contact, and persevere in their pursuit of friendship--skills that are of immeasurable importance considering that host country nationals, having established support groups and being dominant in their surroundings, often do not take the first step in interactions with foreign sojourners (Paige, 1983, p. 123; Roland, 1986, p. 129; Strom, 1988, p. 195; Winter, 1986, p. 327).

Self-esteem shows its positive influence even preceding actual intercultural contact. Thus, sojourners with a high level of confidence about getting along with Americans and optimism about their ability to adapt have been found to befriend Americans more easily than others (Roland, 1986, pp. 121, 126). It has to be mentioned, however, that if the levels of self-esteem reach exaggerated proportions and preclude a realistic and sensitive perception of others, conditions will in all likelihood turn sour--as with any extreme offshoot of something originally positive. Thus, individuals with overwhelming egos at times react to intercultural challenges in a defensive manner and with an inflated self-image not conducive to friendship formation (Winter, 1986, p. 325). Likewise, weak self-esteem has negative consequences in intercultural interactions. Since it usually carries with it anxiety and fears of, for example, negative evaluations by strangers, being subjected to domination, not being able to use English correctly, or receiving blows to one's self-concept (Gudykunst, 1991, pp. 64-65; Strom, 1988, p. 197), a lack of self-esteem often leads to avoidance of contact with strangers and overall withdrawal, or in some cases to an obsessional perseverence with similar negative results (Gudykunst, 1991, p. 107; Du Bois, 1956, p. 40).

Researchers have found that cultural identifiers tend to have less self-esteem than people who are not enmeshed in their home cultures, leaving the question open as to which is the cause and which the effect (Strom, 1988, p. 193). This phenomenon is exacerbated if the home country has a low national status in the host society, often resulting in defensive or chauvinistic attitudes (Bochner, McLeod, & Lin, 1977, p. 279). In general, conditions are most favorable with a combination of high self-esteem, high accorded national status, and low identification with the home culture; the reverse scenario of low self-esteem, low accorded national status, and high identification with the home culture usually leads to little involvement in the new environment and the absence of close host culture relationships (Du Bois, 1956, pp. 117-119).

Friendship Elements

The fourth factor in intercultural friendship formation are elements of friendship. As discussed earlier in this chapter, friendship styles vary intra- as well as interculturally. To summarize, findings point to variations within the United States (e.g., differences between independent, discerning, and acquisitive friendship types, and gender discrepancies); intracultural variations in other cultures are largely unexplored; there are some recurring complaints of sojourners in the United States concerning friendships (e.g., lack of intensity and duration); and noticeable differences exist between friendship patterns in the United States, Germany, India, and Taiwan.

Without reiterating earlier elaborations, a few general observations concerning intercultural friendship formation can be added here. Research literature, of course, agrees that making friends across cultures is more complex since the sojourner is confronted with new and unfamiliar patterns and expectations, and the realization that a behavioral repertoire that worked in the home country has become inefficient (Fahrlander, 1980, p. 17; Mead, 1966, p. 38; National Association of Foreign Student Affairs, 1967, p. 5). To list just one example, Ting-Toomey (1989, p. 360) describes that persons from individualistic cultures are attracted to out-group members with desirable personal attributes, whereas persons from collectivistic cultures look for desirable cultural or social role attributes--a fact that can lead to quite some misunderstanding and alienation if interactants are not aware of it. Apart from the many dissimilarities between friendship patterns and the ensuing difficulties in intercultural contact, however, researchers have uncovered some guidelines that might facilitate the endeavor and unravel the maze. Thus, Argyle & Henderson (1984, pp. 232-234), in a study involving subjects from four locales (Great Britain, Italy, Hong Kong, and Japan), found a set of friendship rules that were endorsed across cultures. The rules are: sharing news of success, showing emotional support, volunteering help in time of need, striving to make the other person happy while in each other's company, trusting and confiding in each other, and standing up for the other person in their absence. Less universal, but still significant were: repaying debts and favors, being tolerant of other friends, not nagging, not criticizing in public, avoiding jealousy or criticism of other relationships, and respecting privacy. The study should be expanded to include a wider selection of cultures, but it does offer a base for discussion.

Research literature agrees that the main function of friendship is homophily. Homophily, again, encompasses similarities with regard to appearance, age, education, residence, social class, economic situation, social status, personality traits, gender, race, marital status, intelligence, opinions, attitudes, values, and interests. Homophily is considered important universally because people in every culture develop self- and role identities through interaction with similar others (Strom 1988, p. 9). Considering findings on dissimilarities between cultures, one could be tempted to presume that homophily stipulations are difficult to fulfill in intercultural contact. However, recent research has shown that attitudinal similarity in friendship formation is a much stronger variable than cultural similarity and even language competence (Kim, H.J., 1991, p. 213).

This finding supports the abovementioned observations concerning the bonding within what was earlier referred to as global ingroups (e.g., people with strong political value systems, unconventional lifestyles, etc.). It also suggests the hypothesis that pronounced and developed persuasions (opinions, attitudes, and values) and strong interests--among others providing the shared and superordinate goals and task-orientation conducive to relationship development (Hammer, 1989, p. 253; Lee & Boster, 1991, p. 191; Paige, 1983, p.109)--override other, less controllable considerations and open the door for meaningful and relatively uncomplicated interactions. Related to the discovered importance of attitudinal similarity is another finding by Gudykunst, Nishida, and Chua (1987, pp. 172-176). The researchers purport that there are four stages of social penetration: orientation, exploratory affective exchange, affective exchange, and stable exchange. Close friendship occurs during the affective and stable exchange stages. Whereas cultural and sociological data play a role during initial contact and often introduce problematic intercultural complexities, cultural dissimilarities have little impact once people move to the friendship stage. In this stage, intra- as well as intercultural interactions have a personalistic focus; i.e., each person is treated uniquely, predictions are based on psychological data, and cultural stereotypes are broken down

(Gudykunst, 1985, pp. 280-281). To conclude, between the existence of at least some universal friendship rules, the bonding potential of people with supercultural similarities, and the correspondence of intra- and intercultural processes at the close friendship stage, intercultural friendships should not be as difficult to initiate and maintain as it has been reported.

Expectations

The fifth factor influencing intercultural friendship formation are expectations concerning the sojourn. The term comprises expectations related to the developmental stages of the sojourners, motivations, and expected outcomes. Corresponding to the intracultural equivalent, the developmental stage of the individual bears significantly on the formation of intercultural friendship. Aspects of homophily such as age, maturity, sophistication, and related lifestyle elements like marital status and the existence of children strongly influence the nature and quantity of host country friendships (National Association for Foreign Student Affairs, 1967, p. 6). Thus, a foreign student in the company of a spouse or family can usually expect to spend a significantly less amount of time with host nationals (Fahrlander, 1980, p. 93), which in turn reduces chances of friendship formation.

Closely related are motivation and expected outcomes. Concerning motivation, we can differentiate between task-oriented and adaptive motivation. Often the main reason for graduate students to go abroad is to obtain a degree or professional training (Bochner, McLeod, & Lin, 1977). Individuals with such a task-orientation usually remain anchored in the home culture and are not immensely concerned about forming friendships with host nationals (Roland, 1986, p. 116). Their antipodes are cross-cultural seekers "who are interested in self-development through interpersonal contact with the host" (Roland, 1986, p. 116). Cross-cultural seekers, on one hand, have more potential for interaction and development of friendships with host nationals (Hull, 1978, p. 57; Paige, 1983, p. 110; Roland, 1986, p. 116); on the other hand, they also are exposed to more stress and frustration when high hopes of contacts do not come true immediately (Roland, 1986, p. 117). Whereas it has been reported that numbers of friends increase during the second sojourn year, first-year levels are usually lower than expected (Fahrlander, 1980, p. 93; Roland, 1986, p. 121).

On a related note, intercultural adjustment and friendship formation are also related to realistic expectations of difficulties (Searle & Ward, 1990, p. 457) and the expected length of sojourn (Hull, 1978, p. 146). Research has reported that while married graduate students from East Asia or Africa are most limited in their host country interactions (Locke, 1988), Western Europeans are comparatively satisfied with this facet of their stay (Hull, 1978, p. 57). Since, in contrast to Asian and African students, Western Europeans often come to the United States primarily to gather cultural experience (Hull, 1978, p. 57), these examples illustrate the extent expectations and motivation influence intercultural interaction.

Adjustment Stage

Closely related to developmental stages, motivation, and expected outcomes but rooted more firmly in the actual sojourn than the individual's predisposition is the sixth factor effecting intercultural friendship formation, adjustment stages. The term is to be understood as an umbrella for two dimensions of adjustment. On one hand, and superimposed on specific sojourn experiences, is the overall development of the individual as an interculturally sensitive being. Bennett (1986) lists six stages in this process: denial (no recognition of difference due to absence of contact), defense (recognition of difference, but resulting in negative evaluations and feelings of superiority), minimization (focus on commonalities with a recognition of only superficial differences, such as food or dress), acceptance (recognition of other culture's beliefs, behaviors, values, and patterns of daily life as viable alternatives), adaptation (empathy and bicultural repertoire), and integration (internalization of different frames of reference, cultural marginality of individual). It has to be noted that the last three stages are defined as ethnorelative with equal footing for diverse cultures; the first three are ethnocentric (i.e., the individual's home culture is central to a reality from which other cultures stray).

Whereas minimization with its focus on commonalities is still considered an ethnocentric stage, it represents a mild side of the phenomenon. Ethnocentrism at its worst is marked by a perception of ingroup superiority, lack of concern and sensitivity for outgroups, avoidance or limitation of interaction with outgroups, or ridicule and outright hostility (Gudykunst, 1991, p. 67). Needless to say, ethnocentric attitudes are not conducive to intercultural friendship formation. To develop close relationships, it is of preeminent importance to accept host nationals on their own terms (Hanvey, 1979, p. 49). Unfortunately, mere contact, even if sustained, will not automatically move individuals to more understanding and the ethnorelative end of the spectrum--as is illustrated by many immigrants and long-term sojourners who, after years, are still separated or isolated from the host culture (e.g., Berry, 1980, p. 14; Dziegielewska, 1988, p. 31; Hanvey, 1979, p. 5). This is true even if the ethnocentric individual encounters a person deviating from the preconceived stereotypes, since such a person is frequently seen as a mere exception to a still-existing rule (e.g., Dziegielewska, 1988, p. 32). To move to the ethnorelative stages of intercultural sensitivity, participation and a readiness to respect and accept are necessary (e.g., Hanvey, 1979, p. 51; Roland, 1986, p. 128); then, time and perhaps special training techniques can bring about a true change.

The second, more tangible dimension of adjustment, is widely known as culture shock. Upon entering a different culture, individuals usually go through several fairly predictable stages of adjustment: the honeymoon stage, during which the sojourner is positively excited and fascinated by the new; a crisis stage marked by complaints, hostility, and refuge with fellow nationals, brought on by the stress and frustration associated with having to live in an unfamiliar environment and interact according to strange rules; a recovery stage with feelings of superiority toward the host country during which composure and a sense of humor are regained; and finally an adjustment stage marked by an ease of communication and the acceptance of host culture ways as just an alternative way of living (Oberg, 1979, pp. 44-45). Evidently the last stage of culture shock corresponds with the acceptance stage of intercultural sensitivity described earlier. It has to be noted, however, that mere contact does not bring on this acceptance. Thus, if a sojourner cannot manage adjustment stress and frustration, is not ready to accept the host culture ways, and does not participate, he or she might not be able to fight through the crisis stage of culture shock and may instead opt for flight and withdrawal, leading to prolonged or indefinite isolation from host country nationals (e.g., Kim, Y. Y., 1991, p. 267).

Cultural Knowledge

Much of the seventh key factor in intercultural friendship formation, cultural knowledge, has been described already in the above section on culture. Thus, cultural knowledge comprises familiarity with the elements of deep culture, including hidden assumptions underlying surface signals, and an ease in using them in daily life (e.g., Kim, Y. Y., 1991, p. 261). Together with language skills, a grasp of the host culture is an essential factor in decreasing misunderstandings and making interpersonal interaction attractive (Gudykunst, 1991, p. 26). Unfortunately, few publications for the United States and even less for many other cultures delve into enough culture-specific details to answer all but the most common questions (Althen, 1983, p. 56). Research is needed to eliminate this problem.

Communicative Competence

The next key factor, communicative competence, is by nature integrally tied to the interaction process and therefore one of the most often mentioned forces influencing sociocultural adjustment and friendship formation. Traditionally, intercultural communicative competence was defined as mere linguistic proficiency. This narrow definition, however, has long been discarded in favor of a more comprehensive picture featuring a wide range of elements.

Thus, Chen (1988, pp. 3-5) differentiates between two dimensions specifically addressing intercultural communicative competence: communication skills and personal attributes, each consisting of a number of separate components. Only the first component of communication skills, message skills, partially resembles the traditional image of foreign language competence. Thus, it comprises verbal language skills, descriptiveness, and comprehension. In addition, however, it extends the original definition to include supportive verbal and nonverbal behavior (e.g., reinforcements, eye contact, head nods, facial expressions, proximics) and other speech communication skills (e.g., effective organization and expression of messages, listening skills, negotiating meaning and clarifications, giving feedback). The other components of communication skills are social skills (e.g., empathy, identity maintainance), flexibility in choosing appropriate behaviors, and interaction management (e.g., turn taking, being attentive, perceptive, and responsive). The second dimension of intercultural communicative competence, personal attributes, includes self-awareness, self-disclosure, a friendly and sincere self-concept, and social relaxation (i.e., low levels of anxiety both verbally and nonverbally). Spitzberg & Hecht (1984, pp. 577-578) add to this list of personal attributes the degree of involvement or expressiveness and other-orientation.

Related, but from a slightly different angle, Hammer (1989, p. 248) divides intercultural communicative competence into culture-specific elements unique to communication practices of a certain culture and culture-general competence which applies to intercultural interactions regardless of the specific culture. Culture-specific elements thereby include all the verbal and nonverbal manifestations of a culture but also the rules and rituals connected with communication. Thus, thought patterns, levels of verbality, amounts of self-disclosure, selection of topics, and choice of conversation partners for specific topics can all vary between cultures (Barnlund, 1979, pp. 98-100). Differences between individualistic and collectivistic cultures are especially pronounced, with language competence in general being more important in individualistic, low context cultures than collectivistic, high context cultures; thought patterns being linear and dichotomous versus nonlinear and holistic; and expressiveness and self-disclosure more or less important depending on the prominence of individuals or groups (Kim, Y. Y., 1991, p. 264; Sanders, Wiseman, & Matz, 1991, p. 95; Saral, 1979, pp. 78-79; Ting-Toomey, 1989, p. 366). Research does point out, however, that while self-disclosure patterns might differ very much during the acquaintance stages of contact, they tend to be comparable in the   more personalized communication of close relationships (Gudykunst, Nishida, & Chua, 1987, pp. 176-177). Culture-general skills include the ability to interact with strangers, deal with misunderstandings, adjust to different communciation styles (Kim, Y. Y., 1991, p. 261) and reduce uncertainty (i.e., describe others' behavior, select accurate interpretations, and predict future conduct) (Gudykunst, 1991, pp. 117, 125).

For effective intercultural communication and the formation of friendships, it is also important to avoid intergroup posturing, which is especially pronounced when cultures have a history of dominance and subjugation and which intensifies and perpetuates ingroup/outgroup problems (Kim, Y. Y., 1991, pp. 266-267). During intergroup posturing, interactions are based on cultural identities and stereotypes, leading to the deindividuation of outgroup members (Lee & Boster, 1991, p. 195). Gudykunst (1991, pp. 20-21) posits that the development of close intercultural relationships is only possible through the exchange of psychological, intimate data and that only this exchange should be considered interpersonal communication. All other communication, such as intergroup communication, is noninterpersonal by definition. On a more phenomenological note, Saral (1979, p. 81) reasons that each culture selects and develops only aspects of human potential, leading to different states of consciousness comparable to maybe the states of normal waking versus dream. The problem of intercultural communication therefore is to gain the awareness and ability to communicate among these various states of consciousness.

No matter which level of perception is taken as a base of operations, research literature agrees that communicative competence plays a superlative role in the establishment of intercultural relationships and that proficiency in the respective skills is one of the major predictors in interpersonal attraction and successful interaction (Lee & Boster, 1991, p. 193; Kim, H. J., 1991, p. 213; Strom, 1988, pp. 168, 197). On a concrete level, in addition to providing the actual link between two interactants, communication competence is indispensable for gathering information about the host culture and therewith facilitating the acquisition of cultural knowledge (Chen, 1988, p. 8). The real or perceived lack of language skills, by contrast, exacerbates fears of making mistakes and often leads nonnative speakers to avoid seeking out, initiating, or prolonging contact (Lee & Boster, 1991, p. 194; The University of Iowa Office of International Education and Services, 1991, p. 49).

External Variables

Adjustment stages, cultural knowledge, and communicative competence represent the main factors influencing friendship formation at the actual sojourn level. Research literature, however, frequently points out a number of minor variables that serve as auxiliaries for sociocultural adjustment. Thus, it is often mentioned that previous transition experiences facilitate adjustment and the establishment of host country relationships (Kim, Y. Y., 1989, p. 278; Paige, 1983, p. 110; Rohrlich & Martin, 1991, p. 164; Yum, 1988, p. 767). Research findings also suggest that socioeconomic status and level of education positively influence interpersonal contact (Li & Yu, 1974, pp. 564, 565). Some correlation has been found too between the degree of interactions, fields of study, and source of support. Thus, foreign students in the humanities and students without scholarships report more contact than others (Hull, 1978, p. 33). Likewise, foreign students with an urban home culture background are said to adjust and interact with more ease than sojourners from rural areas (Du Bois, 1956, p. 52; Rohrlich & Martin, 1991, p. 172). The external variable most often mentioned in research literature, however, refers to gender. Findings are so dispersed, unfortunately, as to be inconclusive. Thus, one study reports that females have more intercultural friendships than males (Heydari, 1988); another merely mentions a higher degree of concern for making friends (Rohrlich & Martin, 1991, p. 171); and a third, investigating social alienation, finds no difference between men and women (Owie, 1982, p. 165). Other researchers note that women in some cultures are not meant to have friends but get their support from kin and neighbors instead (Du Bois, 1974, p. 27). Asian women are educated not to open conversations and initiate contact (Tjioe, 1972, p. 120). This type of cultural background can pose immense obstacles in establishing host country friendships in the United States.

Proximity

The tenth and last of the factors controllable by the foreign sojourner is proximity. Research literature agrees that proximity to host nationals and contact frequency betters the probabilities of positive, intercultural relationships (Paige, 1983, p. 109; Roland, 1986, p. 121; Strom, 1988, p. 10). To create favorable conditions in this respect, living situations in proximity with host nationals or, even better, shared lodging and frequent participation in community and other activities are advisable (Hull, 1978). Unfortunately, institutions at times unwittingly counteract the positive effect of proximity by encouraging or at least not discouraging *international house* type associations in which foreign students live and form friendships with other internationals but not with Americans (Bochner, McLeod, & Lin, 1977, p. 280). Often, sojourners also find it difficult to create the time for frequent contact with Americans, given the time necessary to study and do well in a foreign language and educational situation (National Association for Foreign Student Affairs, 1967, p. 5). As to the most favorable type of contact, if time allows, research findings differ. Whereas the National Association for Foreign Student Affairs in 1967 (p. 6) suggested that informal, unstructured, and natural meetings best promote intercultural friendship formation, the trend nowadays seems to go towards formalized and directed contact experiences. Thus, structured projects like the International Community Workshop, during which foreign students function as learning resources in elementary and secondary schools have been found to positively influence the formation of close relationships (Gudykunst, 1979, p. 186; Paige, 1983, pp. 124-126).

U.S. Elements

Whereas the previous ten factors influencing intercultural friendship formation were at least to some extent controllable or changeable by the foreign student, the last two are givens that cannot be directly manipulated by the sojourner. Thus, U.S. elements are factors rooted in the idiosyncracies of Americans or the status quo of American life that have to be confronted by the foreign student and managed to the best of his or her abilities. Ideal surroundings would, of course, be receptive and favorable toward outgroups and offer plenty of institutional support, providing a fertile ground for intercultural interaction and friendship formation (Fahrlander, 1980, p. 99; Paige, 1983, p. 109; Rohrlich & Martin, 1991, p. 164). Reality in the United States as well as other countries, however, falls short of this ideal, producing a residue of complaints and discontents on part of many sojourners.

As it was noted earlier in this chapter, one of the main sources of foreign student dissatisfaction are the problems encountered in the pursuit of friendship. Americans are seen as friendly but not easy to befriend, too busy and self-absorbed to focus on others, more business- than human-oriented, superficial in their relationships, and indifferent about the existence of foreign students (Dziegielewska, 1988, p. 186; Elenwo, 1988; Roland, 1986, pp. 120-121).

While some of these complaints might reflect the characteristics of highly individualistic societies and the particularities of American friendship patterns, it needs to be pointed out that members of dominant cultures, already having established circles of friends and kin, in general do not seek out intercultural relationships nor find that establishing contact is easy (Paige, 1983, p. 123). This is especially true when outgroup members are seen banding together in conational cohorts or when sojourners appear extremely shy, introverted, and reserved (The University of Iowa Office of International Education and Services, 1991, p. 49; Tjioe, 1972, p. 122). Thus, it is often only during international crises or other international events that attention temporarily turns to sojouners from specific cultures. Too frequently, however, this attention only results in the affirmation of intergroup differences and the presence of stereotypes--resulting, no doubt, from the spirit of competition for resources or superiority which is often the focus of the publicity (Heydari, 1988; Paige, 1983, pp. 109-110; Tjioe, 1972, p. 122). Even if conditions are not conflict-laden and ordinary interaction takes place, Americans frequently relate to foreign students only in their student roles or approach them as cultural representatives in ethnic terms (Bochner, McLeod, & Lin, 1977, p. 279; Strom, 1988, p. 196). As a Nepalese student in a study by Hull (1978, p. 187) succinctly put it: "The foreign student shouldn't be treated like a museum piece." From a foreign student's perspective, Americans then often appear ethnocentric, generally ignorant of other cultures, and disinterested in overcoming their lack of awareness (Roland, 1986, p. 126).

A handbook for foreign students notes in defense that American undergraduate students, especially from rural areas, have virtually no experience with people who are significantly different from themselves and, therefore, tend to be afraid or at least reserved concerning foreign students (The University of Iowa Office of International Education and Services, 1991, p. 49). Graduate students may be more cosmopolitan, but unfortunately often lack the time for social contact. Other population groups that have been found to be more open-minded and interested in interacting with foreign students are people with low church attendance (Heydari, 1988) and students with majors in history, languages, and literature (Shearer, 1965). In addition to culture- or personality-focused complaints, sojourners also frequently point to specific communication problems and comment that Americans should show more sensititvity by adjusting their rate of speech and vocabulary selection, increasing their listening skills, and avoiding paternalisms (such as baby talk or higher volume during communication difficulties) (Strom, 1988, p. 198).

The list of complaints is long and areas of contentment or admiration are often not mentioned or at least not put into print. A closer look at the grievances reveals, however, that whereas some of the complaints are unique to the United States, others seem to be applicable to the intercultural experience of foreign students in general, regardless of the specific host culture. This observation is not to serve as an excuse, however. Thus, with a focus on the future and the improvement of the conditions worldwide, we should promote more cross-cultural education and learn to see sojourners as individuals with varied identities (Spodek, 1983, pp. 89-90; Strom, 1988, p. 196). It also has to be noted that foreign students should not, as they often are, be treated with a double standard (i.e., foreign students are supposed to do well academically, master English, have enough money, behave well, be honest, be quiet politically, be chaste, have no personal problems, live in a particular place after graduation, and do certain kinds of work) (Althen, 1983, pp. 152-155). Double standards and other intergroup attitudes on part of the host nationals set the sojourners apart and thus inhibit intercultural interaction.

Unfortunately, host culture elements influencing friendship formation are the most difficult to alter, especially since there is often no perceived need for change in the host society. It can be assumed or at least hoped, however, that the increasing internationalization of the world and interdependence between cultures will remedy this situation and open the doors for changes even in dominant host cultures.

Chemistry

The last key factor influencing friendship formation is possibly the most important, but also the least tangible. For lack of a better term, we can call it *chemistry*. Chemistry is defined in Webster's (1989, p. 231) as a "strong mutual attraction, attachment, or sympathy," and the usage example given is "matching personalities or some other special chemistry or vibes to make the relationship click." Probably due to its vague and nonphysical nature, the concept has received only minimal attention in the research literature. Thus, only two references with a more or less cursory mention of the subject could be found. Dziegielewska in a phenomenological paper (1988) sketches it as an "invisible bond" (p. 67) and notes that "what draws us into the relationship that deserves the name friendship . . .[is] an interest in the essential person of the other" (p. 59). A more explicit analysis of the concept in its broadest psychical sense is provided by Chang & Holt (1991) in their description of the Buddhist concept *yuan*, or secondary causation. In Buddhist philosophy "any relationship has its roots in uncounted numbers of lifetimes and is situated in a complex web of interdependent causative factors that are outside the control, or even the comprehension of the human mind" (p. 34). Thus, when two individuals meet, their karmic selves, built up through these lifetimes, meet; and it is *yuan* that will determine who will be involved with whom, to what degree, in what kind of relationship, and how long. Having *yuan* with another person means that the conditions are right for the meeting. Out of many contacts, only a few have *yuan*. When there is a lot of *yuan*, the relationship will last for a long time; but even the smallest such encounters are important and might have been prepared for thousands of years. *Yuan*, of course, cannot be forced; one must wait until conditions are right. At the same token, however, two individuals will meet if they are destined to, even if thousands of miles apart. If correct, this Buddhist concept, as well as the similar American notion of chemistry, is thus ultimately responsible for whether a relationship will come to fruition or not. Consequently, even if all other factors are favorable, the final decisive force behind friendship formation lies with the presence or absence of this last intangible factor.

Conclusion

As the intangibility of the last factor *chemistry* shows, it is necessary to remember that a logical and comprehensive compilation of knowledge does not suffice to explain friendship or any other complex concept involving whole beings and their intricate connections and interdependencies (Dziegielewska, 1988, p. 56). As Saral (1979) writes, we need to "free ourselves from our deep rooted addiction to sensing and coding reality in rigid and narrow patterns" (p. 83) and cease occupying ourselves with surface structures and the segmentation of human nature into variables (p. 82). Only if we can focus on cultural experience holistically and the existential linkage between all human beings, can we begin to understand the nature of authentic connection and the true meaning of friendship (Dziegielewska, 1988, pp. 60, 62, 183; Saral, 1979, p. 82).

Chapter 5

Setting and Background of Case Studies

The 15 case studies in the following chapters explore the course and characteristics of intercultural friendships between foreign students and Americans in the United States. Topics covered include the development, maintenance, and deterioration of actual intercultural friendships; the positive and negative experiences inherent in friendships between people with different cultural backgrounds; the peculiarities setting apart intercultural and intracultural friendships; and the individual variables as well as the holistic image characteristic of successful intercultural friendships.

By supplying descriptive information about intercultural friendship patterns, the case studies attempt to increase knowledge and foster awareness about intercultural relations in general, promoting the goal of intercultural understanding and, in the long run, the peaceful coexistence of the world's cultures in the future.

On a more pragmatic level, results may be applied to practice in diverse areas of intercultural contact. For example, foreign student personnel, immigration workers, and intercultural trainers in business and politics might find implications useful in their work. By exposing pertinent questions in the field, the case studies also provide directions for future research.

In the field of foreign language education, findings can be used to further knowledge about the cultures under investigation. In sensitizing our awareness of problems in intercultural interaction, the study also suggests research ideas for more effective communication and language use.

Setting

The case studies took place on the campus of the University of Georgia in Athens, Georgia. The University of Georgia is a state university with a student population of over 25,000--1,286 of which were foreign students at the time of the study in the fall quarter of 1987. Foreign student affairs are handled by the Office of International Services and Programs, an office that provides information and assistance for foreign students and faculty at the University of Georgia, as well as for American students and faculty who are interested in studying, traveling, or working abroad.

Services comprise counseling and advising on immigration matters, guidance concerning university operations and regulations, and assistance with housing and personal matters. Programs provided include orientation sessions for new students and a community friend program (in which foreign students are matched with American volunteers from the community for social activities and support). In the past, the Office of International Services and Programs also offered a campus friend program, matching foreign with American students. This program, however, was discontinued some time after its management was transferred from the office to the students themselves. The reasons for the demise were a loss of interest on part of the student managers, preceded by problems with age difference (interested parties were mainly American undergraduate and foreign graduate students), cultural background (American students requested matches with specific cultures which were not prolific), and divergent levels of demand (more foreign than American students wanted to participate).

Besides the orientation and community friend programs, the Office of International Services and Programs also sponsors events like the

International Coffee Hour (a weekly, informal get-together of foreign and American students), the International Exhibit Day (culture-specific exhibits organized by members of the various foreign student associations as part of a local, annual International Fest), the International Talent Show (music performances, dances, fashion shows, etc.), ethnic focus programs (e.g., Indian Night, African Night, Taste of Thai), family housing activities, and off-campus picnics and tours. In addition, the office supplies advising functions for 26 international groups on campus. These organizations--among others, the German Club, the India Student Association, the Chinese Student Association (Taiwan), and the Student Union of China (mainland China)--sponsor cultural and social activities for their members and the community. The Office of International Services and Programs also keeps a list of translators and speakers available for class visitations or panel discussions. In addition, the university at large provides integrated housing.

Combining all of these above features, the University of Georgia offers a large amount of opportunites for foreign students and Americans to meet informally or in structured contexts. While contact per se is, of course, a necessary first step in friendship formation, is has to be remembered, however, that it does not automatically result in meaningful and intimate intercultural relationships.

Participants

The participants were chosen from the foreign student population at the University of Georgia using purposeful selection to gather a sample that would most likely provide insights and facilitate the expansion of knowledge (Bogdan & Biklen, 1982, p. 67). Thus, only single (i.e., unmarried) graduate students who had been in the United States for a year or longer and who were from Germany (limited to West Germany at the time), India, and Taiwan were considered.

Singleness was chosen as a variable because of the greater amount of opportunity and flexibility that unmarried people have for forming and maintaining friendships. Usually, married people in the early consolidation and childbearing stages of marriage (which would be the time frame for most married students) are preoccupied with their union and family and consequently have fewer friendships than singles (Rubin, 1985, p.118). The friendships that are formed are frequently limited to other couples or to same-sex associations of the individual partners (Rubin, 1985, pp. 119, 133) and are often restrained in the choices of what to do, where to go, or whom to see (Rubin, 1985, p. 132).

The participant population was narrowed to graduate students because friendship formation goes through various stages in the course of a lifetime. Different patterns appear roughly during childhood, adolescence, and adulthood. Since undergraduate students may still be caught in the change between adolescence and adulthood, the pool of participants was confined to graduate students who are mostly in their 20s and 30s and therefore on a stable level of friendship formation.

Participants' length of stay in the United States was set to have been a year or longer at the time of the study to allow for enough time to make friends in the new surroundings. Research literature has shown that whereas first-year levels of friendships are usually low, they do increase during the second year of sojourn (Fahrlander, 1980, p. 93; Roland, 1986, p. 121).

To compare intercultural friendship patterns of people with diverse backgrounds but to still keep dimensions at a manageable level, three countries were selected as a pool for potential participants. The decision to choose the countries of Germany, India, and Taiwan was influenced by the foreign student composition at the University of Georgia, the desire for diversity, and the availability of literature on friendship patterns in the potential cultures. As of fall quarter 1987, the University of Georgia had 1,286 foreign students, approximately two thirds of which, 857, were graduate students. Of the 107 represented countries, 17 had contingents of 20 or more students. After inspecting student demographics of these 17 countries and subtracting from each pool undergraduate students, married students, and single graduate students who had been in the United States for less than a year, it became apparent that only the countries with contingents of 50 or more students provided reasonably sufficient numbers of potential participants to ensure a large enough final sample for the study. When the 7 countries with contingents of 50 or more students were grouped according to relative cultural similarity, three general clusters emerged: countries with European heritage (Canada, United Kingdom, Germany), South Asia (India), and East Asia (Taiwan, Korea, China). For the study, one country was selected from each cluster.

Of the countries with European heritage, Canada and the United Kingdom were excluded as being too close to the United States in their cultural background. Thus, Germany was chosen as the country from this group. (At the time of the study, Germany was still divided, and no change in this status was indicated. All students in the study were from West Germany). India was included in the study as the only country from South Asia. Within the East Asian group, Taiwan was most suitable because it supplied the largest foreign student contingent at the University of Georgia, and literature on Chinese culture is more plentiful than on Korean culture. Mainland China might have been attractive since it is politically more exotic than Taiwan; however, the political factor also entails disadvantages that ultimately caused mainland China to be ruled out as a country of origin. Both the Cultural Revolution and the opening of China to the West with the ensuing influx of mainland Chinese students to United States campuses at the time of the study were fairly new phenomena that were likely to be accompanied by instabilities and changes within China as well as a mutual cautiousness between mainland Chinese and Americans. As has been mentioned in the previous chapter, international political events and crises draw attention to the respective cultures and may skew normal interaction patterns. Had the study been conducted more recently, for example, during or after the events at Tiananmen Square, these effects certainly would have been further exacerbated. International upheaval and its influence on intercultural interaction might be an interesting topic for a separate research project, but it was not conducive to this study which tried to eliminate unnecessary variables, among others by focusing on intercultural friendship between interactants from fairly settled countries.

As of fall quarter 1987, the number of single graduate students from Germany, India, and Taiwan having been in the United States for a year or longer came to 128 students, with 20 students from Germany, 29 students from India, and 79 students from Taiwan. The addresses of all members of the population were obtained from International Services and Programs at the University of Georgia, and explanatory letters as well as a demographic questionnaire were sent to each of the 128 individuals. Addressees were asked to fill out and return the questionnaire if they were willing to participate in the main part of the study, which consisted of an in-depth interview.

Of the 128 addressees, 17 students returned the questionnaire, thus indicating interest in the study. Five of these potential interviewees were German, five Indian, and seven Taiwanese. Since the prestudy plan called for 12-18 participants, with 4-6 coming from each country--the number was suitable for the purposes of the study. All 17 respondents were contacted so that time and place for interviews could be arranged. As it turned out, two of the Taiwanese students were in the process of moving to another city and back to Taiwan respectively and, therefore, unavailable for in-depth interviews. Thus, by coincidence, the original pool of potential participants furnished an evenly distributed final sample of 5 interviewees per country.

Of the 15 participants, 9 were male and 6 female (with at least one female per country). The average age was 28 years and the average length of stay in the United States at the time of the study 2 years and 9 months. The majors of the participants were spread across the spectrum, with 5 students majoring in the sciences, 3 in business, 2 in languages, 2 in education, 1 in a social science, 1 in journalism, and 1 in pharmacy. Whereas for certain research questions it might have been desirable to have a more homogenous sample (e.g., of only female students in the humanities), concerning the exploratory nature of this study, the wide and fairly even distribution within the group of informants presented a very attractive base of operations and the prospect of tapping into some interesting variation.

Data Collection

Data were collected in the form of a questionnaire and an in-depth interview with each participant. The questionnaire was structured in format, consisting of 53 check or short-answer questions; space for additional comments was provided. The questions were derived from concepts surfacing in the research literature and experiential data (see Appendix A).

An in-depth interview was conducted with each of the respondents who had completed and returned the questionnaire. The interview was in the semi-structured interview guide format; i.e., general topics were provided and questions were outlined but the interviewer was free to explore and probe when need arose, to ask questions spontaneously, and to establish a conversational style within each topic (Patton, 1980, p. 200). Like the questionnaire, the interview guide, consisting of 41 core questions, was developed using topics emerging from the research literature as well as experiential data. It differed from the questionnaire in format and contents by focusing on open-ended questions requiring detailed and elaborated responses (see Appendix B).

Most of the interviews took place in the homes of the participants (dorm rooms and apartments). The exceptions were one interview conducted in a group room in a dormitory and two in my apartment. All times and places were arranged according to the participants' convenience to ensure a relaxed and informal atmosphere. Interviews were conducted in English, recorded with the permission of the participants, and lasted an average of two hours.

The interviews were to afford an in-depth look at the participants' friendship experiences with Americans. They also drew comparisons between the participants' intracultural friendships in their native countries and their intercultural friendships with Americans in the United States as well as touch on the participants' friendships with non-Americans in the United States. (For more information on research design, researcher's characteristics, and data analysis methods, see Appendix C.)

Chapter 6

German-American Friendship Experiences: Five Case Studies

Of the five participating Germans, two were female (Marlene and Sabine) and three male (Reinhold, Erich, and Arnold). Their ages ranged from 22 to 27. All of them had extensive traveling experience in Europe, and four had been in the United States previously.

Please note that the names of all participants were changed and that vocabulary or grammar errors were not corrected in quoted statements of the informants. The case studies are reported in the present tense; the reference point for mentioned time or dates is the interview with the participants.

Marlene

Marlene is from a medium-sized town in the North of Germany. Like her fellow nationals, she has traveled widely in Europe, but she is the only German participant who had not visited the United States prior to this sojourn. She came to the United States approximately two and a half years ago to study and work as a teaching assistant in the German Department of the university. Her studies are almost finished, and she is planning to return home in three months.

Marlene has an outgoing personality, is self-assured, and very active socially, being involved with fellow nationals due to her departmental affiliation, as a member of the German Club (the local German student association), and in her leisure time. Spending approximately 15 hours per week with Americans--one of the largest amounts reported among all participants--Marlene has plenty of American contacts. Thus, she lives off campus, has an American roommate and friendly relations with her neighbors, spends time with Americans at work, participates in sports, and takes part in many other social activities (attending concerts, cooking together, going out, and the like). Having only a slight accent and making few grammatical errors, Marlene's English is very good. She, in fact, is extraordinarily articulate, talkative, eager to share her thoughts, and gesticulates freely to highlight her utterances.

Marlene is interested in the arts (especially dance, theater, music, and literature) and likes to talk about related issues and other intellectual topics such as politics and psychology ("I like to discuss personalities"). Thus, during the interview she seemed in her element analyzing friendships and relationships.

Marlene defines close friendship as a state where two people are completely open and share everything--happy moments as well as problems. Close friendship, as opposed to casual friendship, is based on this in-depth communication and requires an honesty that is marked not just by the absence of lies but also by receiving and handing out what seems a good measure of criticism for faults and undesirable behavior. Marlene feels that her definition of close friendship is shared by some but not all Germans. "This going into details in relationships . . . sharing every kind of idea, I think that's not what everybody expects." She assumes that people who work eight hours a day "don't want to sit and discuss things in the evening. Instead, they prefer to go out, have a drink, and do fun activities." She feels that it is mainly the university educated intellectuals who are not satisfied with mere activities but strive for this exchange of ideas.

Marlene says she has four close friends, three of which are German (two females, one male) and one from Singapore (female), with these friendships ranging in length from long-term (10 and 15 years) to ones more recently formed in the United States. While she is in all respects very similar to two of these friends ("even our apartments look alike"), the other two are different in some significant way. Marlene says she likes to learn from other people and develop parts of herself; thus, these friends provide counterpoints to Marlene's conservative lifestyle and politics on one hand, and her extraverted nature on the other. Marlene considers the Singaporean friend, whom she met here but who is now in Germany, her best friend. While she shares everything with all four close friends, the other three sometimes are too dependent and want too much of her time and advice. Marlene likes being independent, and it is only with her Singaporean friend that she has the feeling of two individuals appreciating but not depending on each other.

Unfortunately, Marlene has not met Americans during her stay in the United States who matched her ideals. According to her observations, Americans are friends "as soon as you talk more than 10 sentences," and close friends if you "have been to lunch at least three times." She rephrases in many different ways her perceptions of American friendships as activity-oriented and shallow. She says Americans "are more into activities, they are members of groups, but not real friends" since personal concerns are not shared.

> I noticed that a lot of times when I met Americans, and they asked me to go out for lunch or to stay with them even, you couldn't get that close to them . . . . They ignore or they just don't touch some areas you would like to talk about . . . . And even if you start talking about it, it's just on the surface, it's not going to the real problem. It's stuck at a certain point, and they just don't open themselves.

When this barrier is reached, Americans "have special phrases or patterns they say, and then you just notice they've switched the topic." Marlene feels that not just Germans but "Europeans in general are more open to analyze their own faults, their own problems, their own thoughts. They have more patience to sit down and talk about it." Americans "are not used to hard criticism . . . always polite, polite, polite . . . even if you don't want to hurt them, if you just want to help them . . . they're not able to handle it." In summary, Americans just "don't go into the depth."

Marlene does have plenty of American contacts and singles out five "good friends" with whom she shares a lot of things, goes out, and has fun, but they do not meet her criteria for closeness. Besides the abovementioned lack of openness, Marlene complains that these friends are not as spontaneous as Germans ("You always have to make plans or call before getting together"). In addition, the first one is unreliable ("It's like, let's do something next week, and it will never happen . . . . I wouldn't behave like that to a very close friend"). The second one, a man, adheres to very traditional gender roles and, she assumes, sees her desire to discuss issues and politics as unfeminine ("He's too Georgian"). Her American roommate is fun to go out with but "when it comes to the discussion of problems, it's just lacking;" and another one is not open to share Marlene's interests in classical music and the arts. The fifth friend who, being a former student of hers and Austrian-American, at first filled her with the hope for a relationship with familiar patterns. When the promise did not come to fruition, they actually talked about the issue. The friend explained that she did not like the intensity and seriousness of European conversations: "You just sit, look into each other's eyes, and discuss problems." Marlene, however, counters that "it's just the way of talking that makes it sound like a problem" and that her friend, like many Americans, wants to joke and be entertained primarily.

Whereas Marlene at the beginning of her stay took the perceived lack of closeness personally and thought Americans were not favorably disposed towards her, she now has a more neutral perspective. She says that the absence of close American friends is "not a big concern," and having "very good times with Americans" is satisfying in its way. ("It's just like butterflies; you just go from one place to another.") In conclusion she says:

> I'm a guest here . . . . I can't expect them to have German habits. I myself have to adjust to American habits . . . . The problem is that I still expect too much--coming from a German background--in comparison to what they offer me. I expect more because I know German friendship, and that's why I'm spoiled.

Sabine

Sabine grew up in a village in rural South Germany. She is a microbiology graduate student and lab assistant, and has been in the

United States for one year and eight months. Sabine's studies will be completed in approximately six months; she would like to go to a third country after her stay here.

Sabine is quiet and introverted yet laid back, exuding an air of friendliness, good temper, and patience. Even though her English is good, her speech is hesitant and tentative ("I feel it, but it's difficult to describe"), interspersed with unassuming qualifying statements that guard against generalizations and show intercultural sensitivity.

Sabine defines a close friend as "somebody I can talk to about anything, with whom I can share my innermost secrets, who understands what I'm thinking, and who has some of the same interests." She admits that her reserved nature has made friendship formation difficult at times. "I give up very easily. That's something personal because I'm not very outgoing." For the same reason, she has had problems with openness but has made efforts to change. "If I don't open up to other people, they will never become my friend. It was very hard for me to develop some skills to do this, but it has worked." Her accepting and conciliatory attitudes towards differences between individuals surely must have helped her in this endeavor, with intracultural but especially intercultural friendships. Thus, she reports:

> I like to find out why they live the way they do, why they do things differently. First, it might be curiosity. Then, it's some sort of understanding why somebody is different. And if you understand it and can accept it, then you become friends.

Likewise, her undemanding patience ("pushing makes it worse") helped her once on the way to closeness with an American. "I just left it casual . . . and saw to it that I was available whenever they might need somebody, and I found a very good friend this way."

Sabine has two close American friends, her roommate (female) and a fellow lab assistant (male). She describes her roommate as "very Christian," traditional, and conservative politically. Even though they differ greatly in these values and their friendship has consequently been at times difficult, they are still close due to a mutual understanding in other respects and the roommate's "friendly personality" and helpfulness. Her labmate is more like Sabine in values and interests. She feels very content with the level of closeness in her friendships, since both friends are very open and share their thoughts and problems with Sabine. In fact, it is Sabine who is sometimes "holding back for some reason," presumably due to her abovementioned reserved nature.

Sabine lists four close German friends, one of whom is her best friend who knows the most about her ("We are as intimate as you can get"). When asked about the differences between her German and American friends, Sabine says that her long-term German friendships are deeper simply "because they had a lot of time to develop." Given enough opportunity to interact, her American friendships could grow equally close, especially the one with the more similar labmate.

Concerning the definition of American friendship, Sabine gives two accounts. On one hand, she repeats common perceptions by stating that: "It's very easy to get to a certain point in getting to know somebody, but from then on it's like 'to here and no further.' It's this barrier in a way." She also says that

> Germans spend more time talking together than anything else; the emphasis is more on understanding what's going on with each other's life . . . . Many Americans just don't want to spend a whole evening sitting there and talking together; they want to go out or they want to do something.

Sabine's own personal experiences with her two close American friends, however, do not match this characterization. "They're not average Americans in this respect."

In conclusion, Sabine gives some advice on how to find American friends:

> I would say start with activities, like join a club or do something that you are interested in . . . and you'll find somebody who has the same interests. It's a lot easier to approach Americans that way--do things together first, and then you might get to talk and find out that you are similar in other respects. I think, usually here you don't start out talking; you start out doing things together, and then you might talk.

Reinhold

Reinhold is 22 and the youngest of the participants. His hometown is a large city in the Northwest of Germany. He is a student and teaching assistant in economics, and has been in the United States for one year and seven months. He is not sure as to how long his studies will still last, but is planning to return to Germany afterwards.

Reinhold's English is very good. He seems confident but thoughtful, weighing ideas to arrive at insightful answers and avoid generalizations. When asked about his definition of friendship, Reinhold states that for him a close friend is

> a person you know well, usually have known for several years because it takes a long time to figure out that you can really trust and you can rely on this person. It's somebody you can almost always call or visit and ask him or her to do you a favor. It's somebody you like to be together with and feel safe in his company, or her company.

The issue of trust is crucial to Reinhold. In fact, he suggests testing a potential friend's reliability by asking certain questions or favors "to see how this person would react."

Friendships are important for Reinhold, and he seems to have no problems forming them. Thus, he lists 4 close American friends (all males because of his predominantly male field of studies) and 10 close German friends (males and females), sharing with all of them common interests and ideas. While he calls two of his German friends best friends (one male and one female) because "like a mosaic" some pieces match more than others, he does not rule out the possibility for reaching the same level of closeness with Americans and in general considers close friendships in both cultures the same. "I can't imagine that Americans don't have any problems; I can't imagine that Americans don't like to discuss things out like we do."

Concerning his intercultural friendships with Americans, Reinhold points out: "I can talk to them about my problems like with German friends." He does remark, however, that some Americans are more likely to form intercultural friendships than others. Thus, "Americans who have German ancestors . . . tend to be more interested;" three of his American friends, in fact, have a German background. In describing them, he continues:

> The most important thing is that they showed me they are willing to sit down—especially at the beginning when you weren't as fluent and when you had many more problems not just with the language but also with the environment, with the culture—they could make some time to teach you something. They were willing to help you out.

Reinhold feels that Americans who are open for intercultural friendships tend to "treat you in an equal manner; it's not like they are superior just because they have this language advantage or they know more about America." With the lack of specific cultural knowledge about the United States (e.g., details about past political events, old TV shows, childhood and teenage practices) hindering foreigners' ability to participate fully, these interculturally sensitive Americans "come down to your level so that one can communicate on the same base." Reinhold states that if an American somehow tries "to tell these things [specific cultural knowledge] in such a manner that he [she] invokes an interest in you, and you can respond to it by telling about your experience, then it's much easier to start and become friends." Americans with such a patient predisposition are "willing to listen . . . even if it doesn't make much sense or if it takes a long time to express certain things."

Even though Reinhold considers the quality of close friendships in Germany and the United States equal, he does recognize differences in the concept at large. Thus, he ponders that Americans have fewer close friends because they move so often "they don't spend so much time getting to know somone" and "it's difficult for them to work on a close relationship." If you live somewhere only for a short time, you "want to have fun and don't deal with somebody's problems." Reinhold realizes that the two cultures differ in the width of the term *friend,* with Germans applying it only to close friendships but Americans considering someone a friend "even though they just met him [her] a couple of times." Reinhold describes Americans as more sociable and easy-going, so "it's easier to start a discussion, to start talking." He also recognizes the danger of misinterpreting this scenario.

If a foreigner comes to America, and there are all these people who start talking to you, they seem to invoke the impression that they are very interested in you. And you think 'This is great,' and you just feel very comfortable . . . but then 10 minutes, 15 minutes later you are left alone again. Also, Americans make many promises and then don't keep their promises. This is something that Germans don't do. When you know somebody a little better, you can trust him [her].

Reinhold also remarks on the oftmentioned initial openness but subsequent inaccessibility of Americans. Unlike many sojourners, however, he looks beyond the seeming deficiency. "Americans seem always open but when it comes to personal questions, they always have some barriers, and they don't let everybody in; so that's why they need their close friends, too."

Giving advice to newcomers in the United States, looking for American friends, Reinhold concludes that "they shouldn't be seduced by the friendliness Americans might show; they have to be a little aggressive . . . . It's not like Americans come to you, you have to go to the Americans and then take one of them."

Erich

Erich, from a village in the Rhine Valley, has been in the United States for one year and seven months. He is a student and teaching assistant in applied math science. Erich is planning to return home in two months.

Erich's English is very good and fluent, and he makes the impression of a balanced, worldwise young man with a good sense of humor. His definition of a friend is "somebody who shares a certain perspective of life, who is in my age group . . . somebody I can talk to." Erich feels that most American friendships are also based on a similarity in attitudes and age, but he is "not so sure about this talk-to aspect." Most Americans seem to be "more action-oriented and would consider somebody a close friend who they go ice-skating with twice a week, or they would play basketball with or baseball, things like that." Yet, all of Erich's close American friendships seem to be based on talking in one way or another.

Thus, three of his five close friends--who are all men, one being his roommate and the other four in his "male" field of study--are characterized by him as "very intelligent" and "interesting to talk to" because they are well-read and have "thought about a lot of things." Conversations with these three friends center around philosophy, politics, religion (Erich is Roman Catholic), and cultural differences, but do not include personal matters. Giving an explanation for this omission, he singles out one friend and states that "he's not very open in this respect." This is not the case with his remaining two friends, whom Erich describes as "honest" and "considerate." With them "the most important quality of all is that we talk about very substantial personal things rather than philosophical or political things." The fact that not all of his close friendships have to have the element of intimacy is somewhat illuminated by a statement Erich makes about best friends: "I've never had a best friend that you can go to in the middle of the night, things like that . . . but I think that's my personality." Besides addressing his intellectual and emotional side, Erich's five American friends of course also fulfill other needs, with various friends sharing his religious beliefs, his interest in sports (especially soccer and ultimate frisbee), and his international exchange experience.

When asked about differences between his American and German friendships, Erich comments on two factors. For one, he says that in Germany it is "probably easier to relate to a girl without having her as a girlfriend;" he feels there is some restraint concerning cross-gender friendships in the United States. On a more far-reaching level, Erich states that although the quality of his American and German friendships is very similar, it is not quite identical. "I sometimes feel that I still have a closer relationship with somebody from my country, and I still feel that even though we are friends, we're from two different countries and two different backgrounds." Erich singles out an occurrence when he went out with a group of Americans (one of them being a friend of his), and this separateness was especially pronounced: "I got this feeling they're this bunch of close friends, and I'm kind of on the outside." Erich states that the situation would not seem so severe had they invited him again. He also wishes in general that his friend, who was part of the group, would "integrate" him more into the circle. Erich does concede, however, that this lack of effort is mutual and related to the temporariness of his and other foreigners' sojourns. "You don't invest as much, don't risk as much. . . . It's an easy excuse--it's not really worth spending time to pursue this because in half a year I'll be gone anyway."

In conclusion, Erich comments on the question of whether friendships with Americans have negative consequences. (This was in reference to a statement by me, the interviewer, about some tight-knit groups of conationals from other cultures who do not approve of too much outside contact.) Erich remarks that it is quite the opposite with the German foreign students on campus. "If you stick only with your Germans, you are probably considered a narrow-minded patriot who is not able to adapt to his [her] environment."

Arnold

Arnold has been in the United States for almost two years. He is a graduate student and teaching assistant in the German Department. Planning on changing his major to political science, he intends to stay in the United States for at least five more years and is not sure whether he will return home after that.

Arnold has a very energetic nature and can express himself fluently and well in English. In fact, his speech is quite rapid and concise, to the point of, self-admittedly, sounding abrupt at times. Arnold ascribes this phenomenon to his having grown up in Berlin.

> I sometimes mention things in a rather blunt way, as they put it here--that might be because of my Berlin background. If I dislike something or somebody, I say so, and I don't try to cover it up; I say it very straightforward.

Arnold describes a close friend as "somebody you can rely on . . . and share your most inner feelings with." Close friendship is also marked by complete honesty and "the positive knowledge that whenever I'm in trouble or one of them is in trouble, I would try everything to help them out, whatever that might be, and I know they would do the same thing for me." A close friend from an American perspective, according to Arnold, is "somebody you can have a good time with . . . somebody you can share emotions with also, but not necessarily all the time your problems." Thus, Americans have a tendency to "pretend everything's o.k.;" they lack "seriousness" and try to be "constantly funny."

As in some of the other reports by the German students, Arnold's general definition of American friendship does not hold true for his specific relationships. Arnold lists three close American friends (all female). One of these friendships, however, has recently become strained since his friend married, and her jealous husband makes contact difficult, even though there is no reason for jealousy. The other two friends are his Japanese-American girlfriend and the Japanese-American wife of a German friend. Both of them grew up in the United States and consider themselves Americans. Arnold states that these friendships are built on openness, a "mutual personal interest in each other," and "trust." Elaborating on the last element, Arnold says:

> I can trust them .... It's not that we can play racquetball together--I can play with any other guy--but I can trust them. Trust to a certain extent that if you want to be private about whatever it is, you can talk to them, and you know they deal with it in a decent and trustworthy way.

Even though Arnold treasures liberal attitudes in general and mentions several interests that he shares with one or the other of his American or German friends (ranging from politics, books, and movies to good food, cars, and fashion-shopping for women's clothes), he does point out that his friendships are not based on similarity. "I would say that's very often misinterpreted that friends have to be alike .... [Difference] creates some energetic involvement because we both push each other," learning from each other and widening each other's perspective. It has to be noted that Arnold is the only German participant who, on the questionnaire, marked that he was content with the frequency of his American contacts. Explaining during the interview that he likes to have enough time for each individual friend, he states: "I have a hard time believing that you can have 10 friends .... If you have 10 friends, you can't really concentrate on each individual anymore .... If it's a close friendship, it doesn't really matter whether it's 1 or 10 friends."

In all of these respects, Arnold's German friendships have the same qualities. He only remarks on a few differences between Germany and the

United States. Thus, he states: "I have problems to relate to people in my age group here." Being 26, he feels that many Americans his age are childish and occupy themselves with nothing else but "big parties" and "getting trashed constantly." Arnold also notices a difference in cross-gender friendships.

> Whenever I try to be friendly to a woman here . . . it's very easily misinterpreted, and I think maybe it's because of the very conservative structure down here [in the South]. There is that certain expectation that whenever you start something as a man, you want something, and they get ready for it, and I find it very funny once in awhile . . . . German women are a lot more aggressive and more independent.

Arnold also mentions some special characteristics of his best friend in Germany.

> We really have the most in common. He's the most liberal I can think of, and he's my best critic--he never minds criticizing me, and I never mind criticizing him--and he's the only male person I can show affection to, to a certain extent . . . . And between the two of us there is really no limitation whatsoever about what we can talk about.

Arnold states that maybe all four of his close German friendships (three male, one female) are "more intense," but he is quick to add that this is "simply a matter of time," for these friendships have lasted 12 to 15 years each. American friendships, he thinks, would develop similarly given the opportunity; however, often the great mobility in the United States makes lasting and deepening closeness difficult.

At the end of the interview, Arnold ponders what is at the root of attraction between people. Failing to find an answer--other than a reference to illusive chemistry--he concludes: "The bottom line what makes it really click, you don't know, you just don't know."

Culture-Specific Trends

Making generalizations based on a sample of five participants is impossible and not the purpose of qualitative research. Yet, some prominent culture-specific trends seem noteworthy and will be summarized here or related to the research literature reviewed earlier.

To highlight the qualities of the sample first, all participants could be described as analytical and self-aware. Without exception, they provided insightful and well-articulated contributions. Questionnaire results showed that although all but one (Arnold) did wish for more contact with Americans (especially in areas of discussions, political activities, holidays, and close friendships), they did spend more time with Americans than with Germans and spoke English not only fluently but also more often than their native language. (The ratio hereby was 60% to 40% on the average.) With the exception of Sabine, the participants were on the extraverted end of the spectrum and seemed to have few problems establishing relationships. While they differed in interests, all of the participants considered themselves very political. Their mostly liberal orientation thereby (the only exception was Marlene) clashed in repeated cases with more conservative attitudes of some friends, at times also resulting in their being labeled anti-American. All participants seemed independent and individualistic, perceiving it positive not to band together with fellow nationals. The German participants as a whole had the largest number of close American friends among the sample.

One of the most basic observations concerning American and German friendship patterns is the linguistic relationship between the English word *friend* and the German equivalent *Freund*. With the German term having a narrower connotation, referring to close friends exclusively, many German sojourners are confronted with a stumbling block that causes much confusion and limitless debates. Thus, when asked about the American definition of *friend* and an account of actual friendship experiences, most of the interviewees (except for Marlene) contradicted themselves by referring to the broad meaning of the term for the definition but describing only their close friendships (in the German sense of the word) in relating their actual experiences. Thus, the repeated characterization of American friendships as shallow, short-term, and activity-oriented presumably applies mainly to casual friendships. The distinction between close and casual friendship, however, is vague and further blurred by the mobility patterns in the United States. As Arnold puts it: "It's hard to tell [who is a close friend] because people are constantly moving." Another explanation for the discrepancy between definition and actual experience would be, of course, that the participants, as some of them maintained, in fact did seek out and find atypical, nonaverage Americans to befriend.

Concerning the characteristics of close friendship, the consensus was that "talking about everything" is essential. This factor does entail discussing intellectual issues of interest (favorite topics seem to be politics and philosophy) but more importantly being completely open and honest (not excluding criticism) and sharing one's innermost feelings. Trust, reliability, and helpfulness are self-understood by-products of this openness. While common values and interests were mentioned as ingredients of close friendship, they did not seem to be requisites and, in general, took the backseat to "understanding what's going on with each other's life," as Sabine puts it. The long duration of many of the participants' friendships seems to go hand in hand with this focus, as does the importance of "working on a relationship," which was mentioned repeatedly.

When comparing the findings of this section with the research literature on Germany reviewed earlier, two details are notable. For one, cross-gender friendships seemed to be a common experience, with American and German men and women exhibiting a fairly equivalent amount of openness and sharing of personal matters. Several participants mentioned, however, that the sexes in cross-gender friendships are more equal in Germany, making friendships between men and women--regardless of sexual orientation--more common and uncomplicated than in the United States. This observation seems to be in direct contrast to Hofstede's (1986, pp. 308-310) finding that Germany is the more masculine culture; i.e., that it has more clearly defined sex roles than the United States.

Lewin's (1948) model of the culture-specific distribution of public and private personality layers, on the other hand, was confirmed. Thus, most of the participants remarked on the invisible American barrier to closeness. Interestingly, only one interviewee (Reinhold) recognized that this barrier, albeit further from the outside layer than in Germans, is not an impenetrable obstacle but merely a threshold to a more profound closeness, comparable to similar thresholds in other cultures. As described earlier in this study, the relatively extensive public layers but small-sized private layer in the United States is in direct relation to the compartmentalization of friends according to interests, shallowness of more casual contact, minor latitude of morals and opinions, and permeable insider/outsider boundaries in groups. All of these factors were inadvertently touched upon by the interviewees, including the last factor which caused not only Erich but also Reinhold to feel like outsiders when they were with groups of Americans. In German fashion, they perceived strong boundaries and desired integrative help from their friends. The American group members, however, did probably not realize there was a demarcation line and expected the Germans to initiate their own inclusion.

Chapter 7

Indian-American Friendship Experiences: Five Case Studies

Of the five participants from India, one was female (Madhuri) and four male (Shyam, Hormazd, Deepak, and Vinod). Their ages ranged from 24 to 28. None of the Indian participants had been in the United States before, and only two had traveled to other countries previously (Hormazd and Deepak).

Madhuri

Madhuri is from Bombay and has a medium-dark complexion. (This fact is mentioned because Madhuri later makes a comment about racial relations.) She is a graduate student and teaching assistant in business administration. Madhuri came to the United States more than two and a half years ago and is planning on staying for several more years to finish her studies and gain work experience. Often feeling homesick, she will return to India after this sojourn.

Madhuri is self-admittedly introverted, spending much of her time by herself, playing the violin, for example. Madhuri's native language is English. However, having a taciturn nature, her answers are often short and uncertain, making hers one of the shortest interviews.

Madhuri defines a close friend as a person with similar values and a similar personality (e.g., "I don't like to push anybody around and don't want friends who do either"). For Madhuri, common interests do not play an important role. "I don't know that activities help all that much because some of my friends back home, we're as different as black and white."

When asked about the differences between close friendships in India and the United States, Madhuri remarks, along with many other interviewees, that "American friendships tend to be a lot more casual," and that the average American seems to have fewer close friends (one or two as compared to five or six for Indians). Madhuri also mentions that American friendships appear "more transient . . . . As long as you're together, the friendship exists, after that, it fades away." She explains: "You have a lot less mobility in India than in America, so friendships tend to be more lasting." Madhuri argues, however, that even if physical distance separates friends, friendships in India tend to survive. As another difference she states that cross-gender friendships are more "common in the United States," with Indians being "much more traditional" in this respect.

Unfortunately, Madhuri's observations are not based on personal experiences. She regrets having no close friends in the United States, only back in India. She has some satisfying contacts with internationals here, but she does not consider them close friends. Madhuri would like to find close friends, especially since she will be staying here for several more years.

> When you come to another country, part of your feeling comfortable there is making friends, and until you do, you don't feel absolutely at home there. As long as I thought I was just going to go home after I finished my degree, I didn't feel that bad about not having good friends here, but once I decided that I needed to stay and work a few years, then you would like to have friends around here . . . to feel accepted . . . and have somebody to talk to."

Madhuri gives possible reasons for her lack of close American friends. Thus, she concedes that her introversion might be partially accountable, even though at home she "always managed to have friends." In addition, as a serious student, she has not had the time to focus on friendship.

("It's difficult to get involved with other activities while you are a student.")
While these reasons are her responsibility, the most influential obstacle,
she feels, is caused by racist and ethnocentric attitudes in U.S. society. She
elaborates:

> My understanding of Americans, especially in the South, is that they tend to
> be--I don't want to say racist--but definitely very clannish . . . . In fact, when
> I got admission to Georgia, my brother said: 'You don't want to go there,
> you're going to have problems.' And a lot of Americans I have come across
> have shown some evidence of ethnocentricity. I think that's one of the
> reasons, people are not willing to accept another culture.

Madhuri has heard that Americans from regions other than the South are
"more friendly, accepting, and enlightened. . . . I haven't lived in any other
place in the United States, so it might not be a fair comparison, but I have
friends living all over, and they seem to get along fine."

Madhuri's philosophy of friendship formation is to just "let it happen."
She does, however, have some suggestions on how the university could
help foreign students by providing more conducive opportunities. Thus,
she wishes that the family friend program were more extensive. "When we
came . . . we were asked whether we would like a friendship family, and I
asked for it a couple of times, but I've never been allotted a family." She
also observed that "at a lot of the international gatherings we tend to have
a lot more international people than Americans. That doesn't really
promote friendship." As a possible source for more Americans, she
suggests tapping into the pool of businesspeople and professionals in the
community.

Shyam

Shyam is a graduate student from New Delhi and a teaching assistant in
management science. He has been in the United States for almost four
years and is undecided whether to stay here or return to India. Shyam got
married to a Greek wife a week before the interview. This fact was unkown
to the interviewer, but since it happened so recently, was not considered an
exception to the condition of singlehood in the sample.

Shyam is the only practicing Hindu of all five Indian participants and lists his native language as Hindi. His English, however, is excellent, having had it for 12 years in school. Shyam makes a friendly and sincere impression and is overall content with his stay in the United States.

Shyam defines a friend as "somebody with whom you have good rapport, somebody you can confide in, . . . ask for help if you're in trouble, and have a good time with." In general, no difference exists between American and Indian friendships, except for the tendency that "Americans have a lot of casual friends but fewer close friends." Shyam explains this observation:

> Americans as people are more independent, so there is a different approach. They try to have a lot of friends; they don't meet the same people again and again all the time . . . . In India close friends are together most of the time, day after day after day hang out together. My impression is, Americans probably don't do that; they try to meet different people.

Shyam says that he has three close Indian and one close American friend (all male). He met his Indian friends at college in New Delhi, where they mainly did things together as a group (e.g., go out, see movies, play tennis). They all share a similar background concerning ethnicity, parents' occupation, and economic status, and have many interests and "objectives" in common. Thus, all three of his friends are at present studying in the United States, two of them up North, but one right here in Athens. Even though Shyam discusses a variety of topics with these friends and they talk about external events in their lives, neither with them nor with his American friends does he share highly personal matters. "Other than that," he concedes, they are "very close."

Shyam's American friend used to be the resident manager in his apartment complex. He describes this friend as a "very friendly person," widely interested and conscious of international events, who introduced him to "things American." Thus, they have gone fishing together, had barbecues, gone to music clubs, and watched typically American sports. Shyam says about this friendship, as an example for friendships with Americans in general:

It helped me understand a lot of things, and I started taking interest . . . .
Before that, I did not know a lot about American culture. Then, I had an
opportunity to find out . . . . So, I got a sort of insider's view of the situation.
. . . It's a distinct advantage having American friends.

Even though he is "very happy" with the American friendship he has,
Shyam wishes he had more friends. However, he is very busy in school and
does not have much time. For students who have more leisure but still
have problems making friends, he has the following advice "Some people
come with a very reserved attitude, not opening up. I would advise them
to take the opportunity and go and meet people, go to parties, go to social
activities, and talk to people, not just sit at home."

Hormazd

Hormazd is from Bombay. He has been in the United States for almost
two years, studying journalism. After he finishes his degree, he wants to
remain and work in the United States for an indefinite amount of time.

Hormazd is one of the two Indians who has extensive travel experience.
Many of his trips have taken him to relatives who he says live "all over the
world." Hormazd does seem very well-educated, knowledgeable about
world affairs, and sensitive concerning intercultural issues. He exudes an
air of relaxation, confidence, and good humor. His English is the best of all
interviewees. In fact, in addition to being very insightful, his responses
flow out so smoothly and well-articulated that the interview resembles a
prepared speech rather than a series of impromptu statements. It is for this
reason that much of it will be quoted below.

Hormazd is the only very light-skinned Indian participant, a fact maybe
due to his unusual ancestry, for he is one of only about 100,000
Zoroastrians worldwide. He explains that the Zoroastrians, or Parsis, are
an ethnic and religious group who had to leave their homeland in
present-day Iran 1,000 years ago due to the advent of Islam. Their creed
is "good words, good deeds, and good thoughts," which Hormazd tries to
emulate in his way of life.

Close friendship for Hormazd means "trust, warmth, sharing, being faithful, being very much at ease with that person . . . and knowing that person so well that that person would almost be part of your own family . . . . You could just walk into that person's place and feel like in your own house." For Hormazd, close friends are very important; they "make your life complete." Hormazd describes himself as a listener and private person who does not usually feel the need to share his whole life with people. "I've only one friend back in India with whom I can talk about everything, and even then, not quite. There's always one part of me which I'll keep to myself." Having a talent for helping people, disclosure patterns in his friendships are at times unequal. Thus, referring to the situation with his two close American friends--a classmate (female) and a former dormmate (male)--who "need somebody to be with" and tell him everything, Hormazd states half-jokingly: "In a way, I'm their psychologist really." Asked what aided the friendship formation with these two Americans, he explains:

They showed an interest in me . . . they just wanted to know. That in itself is kind of rare, because kids over here don't really care. They don't care what happens here in the States or around the world . . . . There's a total lack of interest. But when you meet somebody who has no idea but who would like to learn, and they want to share things, and they see the same things in you, that is when you click.

In addition, Hormazd states that he is "not the true case of the average Indian," since--with his parents having lived in London for eight years--his "family back in India is quite Westernized," a fact that contributes to accessibility on his side. At the root of interpersonal attraction, however, is a far more powerful factor. Thus, it is Hormazd's belief that individuals through the process of reincarnation are linked together beyond this lifetime and that good (or bad) relationships are thereby prepared and meant to be. This connection usually remains "at a fairly subconscious level," but with enough sensitivity it can be felt when we meet people. It is for this superordinate cause that common interests or values do not play a decisive role in friendship formation. Hormazd has three close friends in India (one female, two male) and the certain knowledge that he shared past lives with at least one of them.

Hormazd believes that the number of close friends a person has is similar across cultures; the quality of those close friendships, however, differs. Elaborating on Indian friendship patterns, he states:

> You can't really compare the friendships I made here and the ones I made back home because I've been here only for two years and because it takes time to work at friendships; I've had about 20 odd years back home and only two years here. At the same time, I think people have more time for friends because the way of life is not as fast-paced . . . . You can do things with your friends . . . . You're expected in a way to be more than surface friends. Friendship over there, I mean really true, deep friendship is for your whole life. It's not something you can keep three or five years and then say 'O.k., that's it; I'm ready to get out.' It's like, you choose your circle of friends, but then you expect that they be true to you and you in turn faithful to them. It can be a bit too intense sometimes--that's the other side of the coin, I guess . . . . You can feel a sense of suffocation. There sometimes doesn't exist the choice of having your own space as we have over here . . . . that's one point which I don't really care so much for. You have to tell your friend what you've been doing, who you've been seeing, especially if they're part of the same circle . . . . It's like you have to do things with the same people all the time . . . whereas over here, you can have your gang but at the same time you can have friends of your own, and you don't always have to be together.

Hormazd explains that doing things in groups or "gangs," as he calls them, is predetermined by the very close-knit family structure in India which allows you to "stay with your family for your whole life, . . . just be part of that [family], and feel warm." These family ties can also be constricting, however.

> You have to do things for them [your relatives] just because they're part of your family . . . . So, to a certain extent, it's a bit enforced. Now, my own family is not like that . . . . We're close but we don't hold each other in. But I've seen my friends, and they stay in huge joint families where aunts and uncles and parents all stay in a huge house together . . . . You have to smile and be nice all the time just because you're forced to live together.

Whereas in India this closeness of the family and also friendship circles encourages asking for help and exchanging favors, in the United States, "each person fends for himself [herself]."

> Over here, you have to get your own job, you have to leave home . . . you have to show your parents 'Yes, I can be on my own two feet.' It's like, 'since I have to be concerned about myself, I can't give you all that you want.'

Thus, there seems to be more sharing in India, "not sharing of things, but sharing of self." As a friend, you also have the "full power or right to call me whenever you want . . . and take from me." Somewhat related to this greater sense of sharing might also be the fact that "back in India, whether you're a man or woman, you always want to feel or touch people . . . . You can't do that over here, you can't touch men over here." He mentions an occurrence when he sat next to a male American friend and in conversation put his hand on this friend's knee. For him it was merely a coincidental gesture without sexual connotations; his American friend, however, was rather surprised if not taken aback. Hormazd hypothesizes:

> We have a really old history which dates back to about 5,000 years if not more. This place is so new . . . . Because they had to build it from scratch over here, there's a self-interest which is always the main drive. Back in India, there also you do the best you can, but at the same time you're linked to those you meet.

Hormazd perceives a "defense" or "shell" that each person keeps in the United States and hinders them to completely relax and be truly informal.

> I see them with each other; even though they're very close, there's a certain kind of shield that comes in the way, which I don't see with my friends back home. . . . I think people in the States are a bit self-conscious when it comes to showing their warmth and love to each other. There's a feeling that sentimentality shouldn't be there, it shouldn't be too sappy, you shouldn't cling. I sense that even when you're in love with somebody, it's not the same as being in love back in India. It's just the feeling that something's being there in the way. 'It's like, we want to be in love, we

want to be very close friends, but I still have my own goals, my own aims, and I don't have to be reached. And if you are there with me, in love with me, in a way you have to compete with those goals I want to reach.'

Hormazd also reflects on the relatively short duration of many American friendships and the broad category width of the term *friend* in the United States.

'Let's not think of years and years ahead, let's just think of here and now .... We're in school for two, three years together, fine we're friends. But then when you leave, who cares really if we do meet again.' They just find a new friend. The Americans are very nice . . . friendly, but this friendliness which is so easily seen can at times smack of a certain superficiality, which I'm not saying is wrong--because I guess if it works for them, it works for them--but to me, I'm coming from a way that is more old-fashioned, that's still steeped in ways that have been going on for thousands of years. It can be a bit unsettling at first to know that when someone smiles or when someone says that they're your friend, that doesn't have the same meaning. And even though you've been warned about it and you know what to expect, when it actually happens to you, it can be a slight shock.

Students, however, should not let definition and other problems stand in the way of looking for friends. Thus, in conclusion, Hormazd comments on the fact that many Indian students "shut themselves off and then complain" about the lack of American contacts. Hormazd maintains that

they are to blame for it .... They're just part of a clan, they just clique together. They don't have a need to reach out, or if they do, they're too shy, too self-conscious, . . . or too scared of the whole group reaction.

Hormazd explains that some Indians feel inferior when they come to the United States because of their speech accent and because of the third-world status of their home country, making their seclusion somewhat understandable.

If you have been labeled in your mind, you act that way, too. That's something you got to fight against .... We should learn to step forward, but some don't. They stay here eight years, and they don't really have friends."

Hormazd also observes that, to hide their feelings of inferiority, many foreign students revert to acting superior--a fact further hindering intercultural interaction. Describing himself as an atypical student in this respect, Hormazd states: "To me, to be in a place to just study--that's not the only reason why I came to the States. I came to know more people and more about the world."

In addition to not banding together, Hormazd advises fellow Indians in search of American friends to learn to see the American point of view: "Even if you don't think that way of life is what you want to do, at least try to see where they're coming from, know why they are doing that." Finally, he encourages foreign students to actively pursue friendships and not wait for them to happen.

> You can make friends wherever you are if you try hard enough. And you shouldn't really wait to get friends, you should learn to make friends in a way that's not hard-pushing but at the same time not passive. You have to work at it. At the same time you shouldn't want too much from it; you should just get what you can get. There is not one kind of friend; there are all kinds of friends. And even though the ones you got back home are a little more dear because they were there first, you shouldn't let that come in the way of making friends somewhere else, too . . . . If you stay in a new place for five, ten years, you'll find that you'll get the same friends again.

Deepak

Deepak is from Bombay and has been in the United States for almost four years. He is a graduate student in pharmacy and is planning to stay here for four more years of study and work before returning home.

Deepak's native languages are English and Hindi. He seems relaxed and confident in general. Thus, he answers questions about cultural differences and more general topics with ease and fluency. However, either out of amusement or embarrassment, he laughs lightly and is evasive when personal matters and actual friendship experiences come up. Whereas with some people such a reluctance could signify shyness and a need for privacy, in Deepak's case it rather seems to reflect his attitude toward friendship. Thus, he is not sure as to what distinguishes close friends and friends in general and avoids naming and examining individual friendships. Probing deeper, Deepak states that young people in India find friends "around where they live and in the school you go to," and that activities are shared in a group. Thus, you might do sports, go to movies, or have parties with your circle of friends. Deepak concedes that he did have a friend in his group who was closer than the others, maybe a best friend. Deepak quickly adds, however, that "you grow up, too" and that in your adult years you do not "need a real close friend."

Deepak makes   several, at times conflicting, statements about friendship. Thus, he defines a friend as "somebody who is like you" (in viewpoints, for example) and "who has shared experiences with you." Later, he maintains that "everybody is different; you can adjust differently to different people . . . they're all friends." Describing his interaction with the one closer friend of his youth, he states: "It did get personal sometimes, but was pretty superficial other times." When asked who he would contact if he had a problem, he says "everybody I know." In short, the impression is that Deepak takes friendship very lightly and has no great need for special dyadic intimacy.

Tellingly, when commenting on American friendship (which he sees as basically the same as in other cultures), he remarks that Americans seem to do more activities together. Contrary to the common critical reference to action- versus talk-orientation mentioned by other interviewees, Deepak means to make a positive statement.

> I find a lot more people here are a lot more involved in activities whereas at home a large percentage of your time is devoted to subsistence . . . . Here, you have a lot of spare time to do other things besides working.

On the other hand, Deepak argues that "over here, you wouldn't really speak your mind out on everything . . . . Everybody is pretty busy about their own work . . . . People don't have the time to sit down and talk." In general, Deepak is free of criticism for Americans. He   describes   them as "more transparent than the people at home." It is easier for an Indian to adjust here than vice versa; "people are more closed" in India. Americans also are "much more outgoing than a regular person at home. It's much more difficult to get to know somebody at home than over here. So, in that sense, it's much better."

Deepak's American friends are all from his department. Explaining that "as a graduate student you don't have that much time," he states that he does not see these friends much in other contexts; the situation is not different with his Indian or international contacts. However, Deepak maintains that he is content with the frequency and the quality of his relationships in the United States.

Analyzing all of Deepak's statements about himself and his friendships, he appears to be a perfect example of the independent personality type described by Matthews (1986, pp. 33-58). People with this predisposition, like Deepak, are not isolated or unhappy; they also have many contacts, but these contacts resemble more an undifferentiated mass than individuals with potential for very close and intimate friendships.

Reflecting in part the worldview of the independent personality type, Deepak makes the following comment for fellow students in pursuit of friendships:

> Everybody in a sense is going about their own life . . . . People here are not going to get out of their way to come and get to know you, but they are rather open about getting to know you if you go out and try to be friends.

A lot of his conationals, however, "tend to remain very cliquish." Deepak understands that this seclusion is often caused by a "fear of cultural differences, . . . not being able to communicate, . . . being ridiculed, not doing something right, just being different." Even though these fears exist, however, they are not valid excuses for the absence of American friends. Thus, Deepak's advice for someone devoid of contacts is: "I'll tell him [her], it's his [her] problem. He [she] needs to get out and meet people . . . . It's more the attitude than what really happens here."

Vinod

Vinod is from a large city in Southern India and has been in the United States for four and a half years. He is a graduate student and teaching assistant in biochemistry and is planning on remaining in the United States after his studies are completed.

Vinod makes the impression of an uncomplicated, laid-back person with a good sense of humor. His interests are science, politics, books, different kinds of music, "light, entertaining" movies, and cricket. Vinod says that "for all intents and purposes" English is his native language. Even though his mother tongue is Tegulu (a South Indian language), he remembers switching to English very early in his childhood. Vinod is the only participant in this study who, on the questionnaire, marked that he was very satisfied in all the areas of his sojourn: studies, housing, social life, and his stay in the United States in general. Concerning his friendship experiences with Americans in specific, he is happy with the frequency and quality of the contacts. Vinod does not see much difference between close friendship in different cultures, defining a close friend as

> somebody whom you can go out with to restaurants and go to movies, and maybe talk to about their classwork and maybe athletics and sports, and things like that . . . and somebody who would probably help you out if you need help. I guess friends are the same wherever you go.

He also believes that duration is the same across cultures. "If you're friends, you will stay friends, no matter where you live or what you guys do."

Vinod has three close American friends: his girlfriend of four years, a male labmate, and a former female labmate. Whereas he has many things in common and shares everything with his girlfriend, he and the male labmate have--except for liberal politics--"completely different interests," and the one similarity with the former female labmate is that they "have the same sense of humor and constantly crack jokes." (In fact, this friend is now a professional comedian traveling across the United States which, however, has decreased their contact and makes Vinod wonder whether she is consequently "drifting away" as a friend.)

Asked what makes the friendships close, Vinod is uncertain. He and his two lab friends talk and joke about general issues, but highly personal matters are not discussed. Exemplifying the situation with his male friend, Vinod states:

> There are very personal things, like my relationship with my family and my girlfriend, I wouldn't talk to him about, probably not with anybody else. That is a private part of me . . . he also has a private part, obviously he's not going to talk to me about, but that doesn't seem to bother me or him.

Vinod does not "congregate with the Indian organizations" on campus and has not much contact with fellow nationals here. He does remark that a close-knit group of Indians exists who do not look favorably upon too much socialization with Americans. However, Vinod states that "if you come to a different country and you stay with your own countrymen, you might as well have stayed home . . . . Especially if you are planning to stay on, you have to integrate into the society." Vinod explains the fact that this integration has come easy for him:

> I have to admit it to myself, but I think I'm more Westernized than most . . . . Our family wasn't very conservative in the sense of Indian tradition . . . It's not that we ignore Indian culture completely, but my parents exposed us to Western culture. I think that has made a difference.

Vinod lists three close Indian friends, all from his college days in New Delhi and all three male. (Vinod does remark that, unless you are a member of a very liberal social group, cross-gender friendship is not common in India.) As it is frequently the case among Indian college students, these three friends usually met for social activities as part of a larger group. Vinod concedes that he does discuss family matters with these friends but ascribes this difference between his Indian and American friendships mainly to the fact that his Indian friends know his family. Only with one of these friends, his best friend, would he share all personal concerns.

Even though Vinod maintains that close friendships across cultures are the same, he does remark on some differences in friendship patterns:

I seemed to have the impression that friendships in India are deeper, but I don't think that's true. I think Americans just don't express themselves in these terms, and they form friendships that are just as deep or close. I think the way they deal with each other is different. In India friends are often too close; sometimes there's no room to breathe.

Friends in India, for instance can call or visit you at any time and see each other almost every day. They "take a very active interest in your life and your problems and everything, whereas I don't think it's that much here." In the United States "people do things more independently by themselves without necessarily involving their closest friends all the time." Vinod also points out that friendships with people in authority are, in contrast to the United States, impossible in India. "In this country, you can make friends with people like your major professor . . . . That I find much nicer here."

In conclusion, Vinod gives advice to other foreign students who want to find close Americans friends:

I think you have to make the effort, definitely. It's unfortunate, but I think most American students, their experience of foreign students is, most of them don't mix. I think it's up to you to break the ice and make it clear you would like to get to know them.

Culture-Specific Trends

All Indians in this study spoke English with native fluency and only very slight accents. Even though a feeling of inferiority due to speech differences and assigned national status was mentioned as a common problem among Indian students, the Indians in this sample seemed very relaxed and self-confident. With the exception of Madhuri, they were all extraverted, vivacious, and rather individualistic. Describing themselves as atypical, they were not members of an Indian enclave on campus and content with their American contacts. They presented a fairly uncomplicated and at times indiscriminating view of intercultural friendship, with only Hormazd supplying a steady flow of substantial analysis and observation. Again except for Hormazd, the participants considered their studies an almost exclusive priority and seemingly derived pride from a professional attitude that leaves little time for interests or social activities. Thus, the majority of their American friends originated in their departments, and contact was limited. Altogether, however, the Indian students in this sample spent more time with Americans than with fellow nationals (at an average of 60% to 40%); for most of their communication, they used English.

Interestingly, the one element that all the friendship definitions of the Indian participants have in common is that they would not share highly personal matters, except for possibly with one best friend. Besides this factor, having a good time and helping each other in times of need were mentioned several times. Only Hormazd listed more internal qualitites such as trust, warmth, and loyalty. Likewise, only Hormazd observed a variety of specific differences between friendship patterns in the United States and India. Most of the other interviewees maintained that friendships are generally the same. Only one dissimilarity cluster was highlighted, namely that friends in India socialize in groups, spend time together on a daily basis, and may call or visit each other at any time. While it was considered positive that many friendships in India last a lifetime, several of the participants noted that the Indian kind of closeness can be at times suffocating, leaving "no room to breathe." Giving advice to fellow students, the consensus (at least among the male contingent) was to not remain within close-knit Indian support groups, but to make a conscious effort and actively look for American friends.

In addition to the summarized trends above, several questionnaire and interview results reflecting findings in the research literature deserve mentioning. For one, the participants' reports confirm the description of Indian family structure and its effects. Thus, interviewees referred to their families frequently (e.g., stated that they missed them, that close friends are almost like family, that family cohesiveness precedes closeness between friends). The fact that the lack of privacy in Indian family life is said to breed social competence and adaptation skills seems also reflected in the overall satisfaction of the participants. In addition, the secretiveness concerning personal matters could be in direct relation to the uncertainty and distrustfulness outside familiar and all-encompassing kinship ties described in the research literature.

Another detail commented on by one participant is the difference in authoritarianism between the two countries. Thus, Vinod remarked that whereas you can be friends with your major professor here, this is an impossibility in India. Participants also confirmed that cross-gender friendships are traditionally not favored even though they are becoming more common practice nowadays, especially in big cities and "liberal circles." Related to this topic, Hormazd mentioned the accepted physicality between men in India, exemplifying overall intra-gender closeness patterns mentioned in the research literature. It has to be noted, however, that the male participants in this study did not exhibit the described patterns of sharing and rather avoided getting highly personal. In the same vein, descriptions of Indian friendships featuring large amounts of affiliation, nurturance, mutual help, sensitivity, love, and intimacy were only repeated partially (especially by Hormazd). Maybe related to this trend, complaints about American superficialty were only confirmed by Madhuri and in part Hormazd.

One last detail of possible interest is that research literature comments on the ideal of social harmony on one hand and the coexistence of multiple realities on the other. These factors combined often cause Indians to agree on a divergence of opinions or be noncommittal and ambiguous. Indian participants in this study made many qualifying remarks and contradictory statements--a phenomenon quite possibly signifying the above tendencies.

Chapter 8

Taiwanese-American Friendship Experiences: Five Case Studies

Of the five participants from Taiwan, three were female (Chia-Ling, Hsiu-Hui, and Chiu-Mei) and two male (Shih-Ming and Kuo-Hsiang). Their ages ranged from 26 to 38, making them on average the oldest group in the sample. Except for one (Shih-Ming) who had been in the United States for a five-year sojourn previously, none of the Chinese participants had any travel experience outside of Taiwan.

Even though the Taiwanese participants were less proficient in English than the other interviewees, they were without exception fairly fluent and understandable. Thus, most of their deficiencies concerned occasional vocabulary limitations and, although frequent, mostly minor grammatical errors.

Chia-Ling

Chia-Ling is from Taipei and has been in the United States for more than five years. She will return to Taiwan this year, after completing her degree in counseling.

Being with 38 years the oldest of the participants, Chia-Ling gives a very mature and centered impression. Maybe due to her major, she is knowledgeable about interpersonal issues and made many insightful statements. Having graduated from the best schools in Taiwan, her interests are highly intellectual. Thus, she likes discussing politics, world affairs, and philosophy with her friends. Chia-Ling speaks with thoughtful and deliberate expression. Her English is very good, with only a slight accent and sporadic, minor grammar errors.

For Chia-Ling, close friends are people "who have mutual understanding . . . and care about each other." While they can talk about almost everything, they usually do not share highly personal family concerns. They talk "about some things, but not much," dealing with family matters within the family rather than with "outside people." Chia-Ling says that Asians are more intuitive concerning interpersonal relations. Thus, "you just know what the friends need. We don't need them to ask first, we just do for them. Maybe we do secretly, they don't know we try to help them . . . . But in the U.S. I must speak out."

Chia-Ling lists three very close Chinese friends (all female) whom she has known for a long time. Back in Taiwan, they used to meet every day and "really talk about something deeply, maybe philosophical, a life issue, politics." The focus with these three friends has never been doing things together, but caring, sharing, intellectual stimulation, and helping each other understand things more. Asked about the fact that these and apparently all of her other friends are females, Chia-Ling counters that she spent her pre-college years in sex-segregated schools and, therefore, had only female friends. She half-jokingly adds that when she later went to coed college, she was unable to find males who were up to par with her and her friends' "intellectual level."

Chia-Ling is a private person and does not want to bother people with her personal problems. ("If I need help, maybe I would go to a counselor.") This is especially true in the United States, where her two close friends, both her age, female, and students in the Counseling Department, are occupied with their own concerns (one of them just had a divorce, the other one has three children and a job). Except for the sometimes infrequent contact, Chia-Ling feels very content with these friendships. She explains that both are very friendly, interculturally sensitive (having traveled extensively), and reliable (having taken care of her when she recently had surgery). Possible differences in personality and interests, even political views do not matter much for Chia-Ling, since the most important element of friendship, caring, is present. (She jokingly does add at least one similarity about her friend with the three children, however: "We're the same height, so she likes me a lot"--Chia-Ling is fairly small in stature.) When they find time to meet, in dyads or as a group, they mainly just "sit and talk" (about their studies, personal matters, or broader issues of import). Chia-Ling feels very comfortable with her two American friends, explaining: "They treat you like a regular person, not a foreigner. Other people, they are very polite to you, but you don't feel you can close to them." Chia-Ling has a number of other good American contacts besides these two close friends and is overall very content with her social life here. She does concede, however, that due to the temporariness of her stay and her self-contained nature, a less satisfying social life would be no tragedy.

> If people come here is just temporary, it's o.k. not to always have a social life. To me it's not important. I can enjoy myself easily even if I don't go out to see people . . . . Some of my friends say I'm very centered. I never feel empty. I always have lots of things to do.

Commenting on American friendship patterns in general, Chia-Ling notes:

> Americans are more self-centered; they see themselves first, even with friends. But for us, we see others first, we try to see from that person's viewpoint. But Americans think, 'What I do for friends will not affect my well-being.' They won't hurt themselves to help friends. Americans wouldn't do that.

Chia-Ling observes that Americans "need company to kill time" and that she does not think "they talk very deeply." "Sometimes I feel they just talk nonsense--or maybe what I think nonsense, is not nonsense to them, that's their culture. Maybe they like to have more fun, but we're more serious." Elaborating, she adds: "Sometimes I feel they are empty . . . . They work hard all week. When they finish the work, they have nothing . . . . I feel they're emotionally not very stable . . . they easily become very depressed." She also thinks that although Americans "are good to each other, they have distance" and "don't want people to intrude on their lives."

Chia-Ling lists several problem areas potentially inhibiting intercultural friendship formation between Americans and Chinese.

Thus, she comments that while American graduate students are less distant, undergraduate students often shy away from foreign students. She explains: "They don't have too much chance to contact with foreigners, they just come out of high school. They're probably not used to." Chia-Ling also attributes some of the problems to language difficulties. Thus, she states that "it's much easier to talk to a friend from the same culture . . . . You don't need to explain so much and lose the fun part. On the deep level it's hard to explain cross-culturally." Related to this factor is the observation that "Americans are not patient" with Asians who often speak at a slow speed, and that Asians "are not very aggressive," standing up for themselves and insisting on getting heard. Thus, in conclusion, Chia-Ling advises foreign students: "If you need to say something, just go ahead and say, no matter how bad your English is . . . you need courage. Don't be scared. Some people might not be interested in you, but some people, they may want to be friends with you . . . . Try."

Hsiu-Hui

Hsiu-Hui is from Taipei and has been in the United States a little more than one and a half years. She is a student in foreign language education with a focus on English as a second language. Hsiu-Hui will probably return to her home country after her studies.

Maybe due to her major, Hsiu-Hui's English is the best of the Chinese students; she makes only few grammatical errors, has a good vocabulary, and her accent is very slight. Hsiu-Hui speaks deliberately and with a soft voice. She is quiet but confident, elaborating on her statements in a sincere and serious fashion.

For Hsiu-Hui, a friend is someone who is "reliable and considerate" (e.g., keeps promises and secrets). Friends should "share feelings and care about each other. If you need them, they are there, but a friend will not bother you all the time" (e.g., call only to ask questions or favors). Rather, a friend could call just to say: "Hello, I miss you, you were in my dream last night."

Hsiu-Hui has three very close friends in Taiwan who completely match her ideal. She stresses that they have been friends for a very long time and are very reliable. While these friends differ from her in hobbies or personality (e.g., are outgoing, which she is not), they all share an "interest in each other" and want to "learn from each other." Typical times together are spent sharing food and talking about everything. Interaction with them is very "natural" and not forced. Hsiu-Hui says: "We didn't mean to make friends, just be friends." Even though Hsiu-Hui does not socialize much with the close-knit Chinese groups on campus because at many of the meetings people "chat about others . . . and try to dig into your secrets," she does have five good Taiwanese friends on campus (four female and one male, the brother of one of the females) who are different and who she sees frequently.

Hsiu-Hui lists only one close American friend. This friend is a pastor, who is 62 years old, retired, and holds family service in his home. Hsiu-Hui is Christian and attends these services regularly, often staying on afterwards to talk or help in the house. She says that he is like a father to her, and he and his family have taken her in like a daughter. Hsiu-Hui feels very comfortable with this friend because he is very considerate (e.g., regularly asks her about her family), and does not push her ("He lets you decide what you really want, just gives a little help"). She states that he is interested in international issues and other cultures and overall does not seem like a typical American.

> I just could tell from his attitude, the way he talked to me . . . . Everything he said, he promised he would do it. That's the thing I loved, because Americans even if they are older, they say so nicely and they promise you things . . . when you call them, they forgot. And he remembered my name so well. Many Americans could not pronounce my name . . . I know he prayed for me every day . . . . I know he is the kind of person who does things and not always talks. Sometime he offered help; I'm not the kind of person who asks for help, but he offered it.

Unfortunately, Hsiu-Hui has also had disappointing experiences with Americans, even leading her to not trust people from another culture anymore and to "keep distance" at the beginning of a relationship. Thus, she mentions many   occurrences where Americans promised   or suggested something (e.g., a weekend invitation to someone's family) but never followed up on it and never apologized either. She details one situation where she was matched with a community friend family who "just want knowledge and information--'I don't know your culture at all, tell me more, tell me more'--but they are not interested in friendship." Thus, they told her about a lot of interesting places but never took her there. Hsiu-Hui believes that they signed up for the community friend program just to look good in their church. "They think they're Christians, and Christians should offer help. They are liars. When you see them laugh or smile, you can tell it's not genuine."

Hsiu-Hui says she does not have enough knowledge about U.S. culture to define friendship from an American perspective, but she does have some related experiences or observations to share. Thus, her American roommate in the dorm once told her "that she doesn't have friends like I do, very close." Hsiu-Hui feels that Americans "don't know whether they are real friends or not" because so many relationships last only a fairly short time. Hsiu-Hui has also observed that some Americans do not "listen very carefully or close their ears . . . they just want to get things done."

Besides these idiosyncracies of Americans, Hsiu-Hui also mentions some problems foreign students face in making intercultural friends. Thus, she states that she has an interest in massage and acupuncture; but when asked whether she has sought out similarly oriented Americans in the community, she concedes that, because people on the phone have often been rude to her, she is not very active in the search of like-minded individuals she does not know. "It's easy for me to give up; I rather call people I know." Another obstacle in the way of friendship with Americans is that undergraduate students often feel superior and "wouldn't be bothered to talk to people from other countries. They don't even know where the countries are . . . they're more concerned with themselves." Graduate students, on the other hand, are often too busy for outside activities.

Hsiu-Hui says that since she will return to Taiwan soon, she is not concerned about making more American friends, but she advises other foreign student in search of contacts to "go outside, watch and listen to people and what they are talking about . . . and choose people with whom you feel more comfortable, and you might make a friend.   From that friend, you can make more friends . . . just go outside."

Chiu-Mei

Chiu-Mei is from Taipei and a student in instructional technology. She has been in the United States for almost two and a half years and is planning to stay here for another five years until her studies are completed.

Chiu-Mei's English exhibits consistent, moderate grammatical deficiencies but in general is fluent. Her utterances, however, have a slightly breathless and choppy flavor, which possibly reflects her self-admitted general nervousness.

A friend for Chiu-Mei is someone with whom she "can share the feeling, including secrets." Friendship also means accepting "the whole of them," strengths and weaknesses without wanting to change them. Chiu-Mei has a number of very close Chinese friends. Thus, back home she used to meet with a group of four or five women she knew from college. They would get together to share what happened, "share the work experience, the feeling experience, your future plan, and share the personal thinking, and personal secret." In addition, they had a common interest in movies, books, and art. Chiu-Mei also considers her parents and her younger brother very close friends. They have a very good, nourishing relationship and exchange letters almost weekly. Chiu-Mei also has Chinese friends here, one of them being a close friend from Taiwan. Chiu-Mei believes human beings and close friendships are the same in different cultures. However, due to the common language and cultural background, it is easier to make friends and talk with fellow Chinese. ("I'm lazy to make a friend with the different language people I guess.") Chiu-Mei also feels that opportunites to form friendships with Americans are lacking. "I don't have a chance. Everybody just in class . . . and when the class over, everybody just say 'bye-bye.' Seldom to have a chance to make a close."

Yet, Chiu-Mei does have one close American friend, whom she met through one of her Chinese contacts. This friend (a male) has a Brazilian father and thus some international experience. Chiu-Mei feels very comfortable with him; they both share a lot of interests and can talk about everything. In general, Chiu-Mei prefers the company of male to female fellow students. She describes American men as more open-minded and easy-going and has observed that the women here are often too concerned with their appearance. When asked why she has not made more American friends, women or men, Chiu-Mei--in addition to the abovementioned obstacles--relates an interesting personal experience. One of the first people Chiu-Mei met upon entering the United States was her advisor. It has to be noted that Chiu-Mei, who has been interested in the United States all her life, had positive feelings about coming here and, having been an A-student and well-liked by her Chinese teachers, expected her sojourn to be very successful. However, during the first meeting with her advisor, he pointed out that her English is very poor and recommended that she not take a full load of classes. He also refused to sign some sort of recommendation Chiu-Mei needed to get the lease for an apartment in which she was interested, explaining "I never sign these contracts for any student." During her first quarter here, this advisor, who is Chiu-Mei's major professor and who she says is "very funny" with American students but serious with her, also told her "you make me crazy" in front of the whole class when she committed an error. Chiu-Mei concedes that she is sensitive and that this advisor might not mean any harm; nevertheless, she felt treated as less intelligent than she is, not respected in her personality, and as an outsider. Chiu-Mei says: "It really hurt my heart," and that the experience has cast a "big shadow" over the two and a half years of her sojourn, influencing also her motivation to make American friends.

> Maybe I have a narrow mind to make a friendship with Americans because the beginning when I came here, I cannot set a very good relationship between my advisor, so this is the reason . . . because in beginning I failed, and now sometimes I feel no necessary because sometime I don't trust them.

She realizes that she needs to "break through this bottleneck" of not trusting Americans; "it's possible but need time." Only when she can balance her bad feelings with the belief that she can learn from this sojourn will the situation normalize and she can be the happy person she used to be.

Chiu-Mei's deplorable experience might find a partial explanation in what is called *self-shock* in the research literature (Zaharna, 1989). Thus, "for the sojourner, self-shock is the intrusion of inconsistent, conflicting self-images" (Zaharna, 1989, p. 518) caused by the clash of behavioral norms across cultures and hosts' unexpected negative responses to behaviors considered desirable in the sojourner's home culture. "The intercultural challenge is how to maintain consistency and sameness of self in the face of radical behavior change" (Zaharna, 1989, p. 514). Chiu-Mei's remarks "I need to balance myself" and " I'm not like that" illustrate this identity struggle; and the fact that after two and a half years she is still affected by a number of very short and, most likely, basically nonhostile remarks shows how overwhelming this challenge can be.

Shih-Ming

Shih-Ming is from a medium-sized town in the Eastern part of Taiwan and a student of public administration. Shih-Ming has sojourned in the United States twice; this time he has been here for eight years, previously he had stayed five years. Shih-Ming will finish his degree soon but is not sure when he will return to Taiwan.

With 37 years, Shih-Ming is the second-oldest participant. He makes the impression of a person who enjoys life and trusts that all obstacles and problems can be overcome. He describes himself as hard-working but also sociable and always available when someone needs help. The fact that he left home when he was only 14 to go to a good school in the capital of Taiwan, and that from this time on he visited his family only during summer vacation, has made Shih-Ming independent and able to adjust to difficult situations. Shih-Ming is very open and talkative; his English is good and fluent.

For Shih-Ming, the most important characteristic of a close friend is that "when you have some difficulty, he or she can help." He says very close Chinese friendships "last forever" and are so deep that friends would "die for you."

Shih-Ming's friendships in Taiwan, however, have dwindled or faded a little due to his long absence and his infrequent correspondence. He realizes that "friendship will not come out of the sky" and that people have to put in time and energy. Comparing friends with family relationships, Shih-Ming says:

> With a family, even if you don't write to them or talk to them a couple of years, when you need them, you can ask them, no problem. But friendship, if you don't write to them but maybe once a year or two . . . your friendship will come no more--even in Taiwan.

Shih-Ming is involved in the Chinese student organization on campus and helps newcomers and fellow nationals or mainland Chinese in need. Consequently, some of his contacts are Chinese; at least as many if not more, however, are American. Thus, he lists four close American friends (all male), whom he met in the graduate students' dorm or through other friends. These four friends are all different: one of them sharing his interests in outings and sports, one of them having the same sense of humor, one being more a confidant that the others, and the last one being "not tall, also short" and sharing Shih-Ming's love of food. Besides these friends, Shih-Ming seems to have a myriad of other satisfying contacts of whom he says: "They're all good people." One phenomenon Shih-Ming points out is that many of his friends are Christians. He observes that while good people and potential friends can be found among Christians and non-Christians alike, the contingent among Christians seems to be higher (60% as compared to 40% among non-Christians).

When asked about the differences between the United States and Taiwan, Shih-Ming states that his close friendships are basically the same, with mutual help being the most prominent element. In general, however, he does see some differences concerning friendship and other cultural patterns. Thus, he remarks that Americans

> have high mobility. Today they come here, tomorrow they go over there. They always think the future, they never look back in the past. So, they have not so much energy to deal with old friends, so they have to make new friends. That's why their friends cannot make like long-term. I think most their friends cannot make deep . . . . If you want to go further, maybe it's sometimes difficult for you."

Shih-Ming points out that Chinese in general are more other-oriented.

> [Americans] don't care about their parents, they don't care about their brothers; like Chinese, they help each other. Americans, they say 'That' s

his business, not my business.' Their culture emphasizes individualism. You see, like they write the letter, they first write your name, your street, state, and then country. They emphasize individualism. But in China, we write the country, then the last one is you. Everyone is whole; so it's different.

Other-orientedness and mutual assistance also have their effects on financial transactions. Thus, "for an emergency, I can borrow $3,000, $4,000 [from a friend] immediately, no problem. But Americans, no, maybe $10, $20, even your close friend." Unfortunately, Shih-Ming learned about this cultural difference the hard way. A year ago, he lent $2,000 to what he thought was a friend, only to never see the money again. Even though his experience is a drastic example, Shih-Ming believes that Americans generally forget "that you've done them a favor." Another occurrence that puzzled him in connection with other-mindedness happened when he had recently arrived and a professor took him to a restaurant but then did not pay for Shih-Ming's dinner. That, he remarks, would not be possible in Taiwan where teachers take care of their students. On another note, Shih-Ming mentions that "Americans always speak up, but sometimes Chinese, they don't speak up. Maybe out of 10%, they speak up 8%, leave 2% to guess what you're thinking." Related to this observation, he shares part of his secret in adapting to the United States and establishing successful social relations: "I always ask 'What does it mean?' The next time, I understand."

Kuo-Hsiang

Kuo-Hsiang is from Taipei. He is a graduate student and teaching assistant in mathematics and has been in the United States for one year and nine months. He will finish his studies in two to three years and then return home.

Kuo-Hsiang is a very friendly and open person who shares his insights and experiences eagerly. His English is fairly good, even though his speech is halting at times and awash with self-corrections. Kuo-Hsiang has good listening comprehension skills, but his vocabulary has a few limitations and his grammar features consistent errors, which do not hinder understanding, however.

Kuo-Hsiang states that the category width of the term *friend* in Taiwan is fairly broad. "Even though we just met once . . . we can say that person is a friend." A close friend, however, would be defined as "a person who can give you a hand whenever you need . . . share your happiness or sadness." Kuo-Hsiang continues: "I will tell my good friend everything I happened . . . even though I didn't tell my family or my parents." He adds that close friends are "for life" in Taiwan.

Kuo-Hsiang has four close Chinese friends, dating back to his school and college days in Taiwan. All four friends are male. (Kuo-Hsiang points out that cross-gender friendship is possible, but "strange" in Chinese culture.) Kuo-Hsiang is very content with his Chinese friends, all of them being very similar in values and interests. "We have the same idea about everything; I think this is the most important thing to be a good friend." They are so much alike that the three closest ones of his friends are at present also foreign students, two being in the United States and one in Germany. Kuo-Hsiang states that back home he used to meet these friends one on one but also in groups. "I spend most of my time talking . . . sometimes we go out together to see a movie." The topics of their conversations comprise "almost everything." "The most thing we talk is about the study, sometimes we also talking about the private thing--we spend much time talking about the girlfriends--or some everything we think." The one exception in the coverage are highly personal family matters." We talk about the families but not very deeply."

Asked about the American definition of a close friend, Kuo-Hsiang admits that he does not "know so much" about American culture. He has, however, had two experiences which might be related to differences between American and Chinese friendships. Thus, he states: "General Americans will not ask a person about his [her] family . . . . But in my culture, when we met a new friends, we will ask about his [her] family." Kuo-Hsiang got this impression when he asked his American officemate about his background but received only short "yes or no" answers. At another occasion he offered the use of his VCR to his landlady who wanted to watch a TV show that she had missed and he had taped. But she declined, saying that "she would never touch my

VCR if I'm not there." Kuo-Hsiang states: "In my country if we are very good friend each other, I can lend you anything, I can also borrow anything that you have . . . . In America, they will very scare I will make it broken."

Kuo-Hsiang regrets not having any close American friends. In fact, even his casual contacts are rather scarce. Thus, the three Americans closest to him are his officemate, his landlady, and his housemate. Leaving home early in the morning, staying at the office all day, and returning late at night, Kuo-Hsiang's most frequent contact is with his officemate. Their relationship, however, is confined to matters concerning their field of study. "The most time we talk is about mathematics. He never tell me anything about his family and his life." Thus, not knowing about his values or interests, and never seeing him outside the office, he is "just a friend" but not very close. Kuo-Hsiang describes his landlady as an old widow who is very kind and with whom he talks often, "sometimes just about my family or her family." He would not consider her a close friend, however, because "some viewpoint are very different." Kuo-Hsiang's third-closest American contact is his housemate, who moved into an adjacent room one and a half months ago. Kuo-Hsiang concedes that he has only seen him twice so far.

> The first time I met him, he was moving in, . . . and he just introduced himself. (His name is Sean and his major is geography.) . . . The second time is one week ago. It's late night, because I didn't close my door, and when he came back, he just say 'Hi, hello,' that's all.

With these insubstantial relationships being his closest American contacts, it is no wonder that Kuo-Hsiang would like to make more American friends. However, he concedes that since his sojourn is temporary and he does have a support group of fellow nationals here, the situation is endurable. Besides, being busy with his studies, he has severe time limitations. "It's very difficult for me because in my department, there are many assignments, so I have to spend my all time to work with this."

Culture-Specific Trends

The Chinese participants in this study (with the exception of the self-admittedly nervous and unbalanced Chiu-Mei) made extraordinarily mature and equanimous impressions. The women were thereby more soft-spoken and thoughtful, the men more good-natured and extraverted. All of their statements seemed very attentive and sincere. While their English was good with minor deficiencies mainly in grammar, most of them admitted to speaking and interacting in Chinese slightly more than in English (the ratio being 60% to 40% on the average). Of all the participants, the Chinese students had the smallest number of American contacts, and most of them wanted to return to Taiwan after their studies (with only Shih-Ming being undecided).

Concerning the Chinese definition of close friendship, the consensus was that it entails sharing (material matters, ideas, and feelings--except for maybe highly personal family concerns), caring for each other, and helping (even without being asked). Close friends spend most of their time talking together and usually form bonds that last a long time if not for life. Some of the Chinese participants modestly intimated that they did not know enough about American culture but felt that friendship here was not as deep and as long-term. They also remarked that cross-gender friendships were more common and accepted in the United States. The obstacle to intercultural friendship formation mentioned repeatedly were language difficulties, especially when talking about "deep levels" of issues or intimate matters. Thus, the pieces of advice given by the Chinese participants all related to communication (e.g., "If you need to say something . . . don't be scared," "Go outside . . . and listen to people, to what they are talking about," always ask "What does it mean?"). The level of international interest on part of the Americans was singled out as another important factor hindering or aiding the development of friendship. Two participants also mentioned that chances for interactions were lacking, pointing out that after classes everybody just leaves instead of talking and interacting as in Taiwan.

Besides these trends exhibited in the questionnaire and interview findings, many of the participants' statements also found their mirror or explanation in the research literature reviewed earlier. As with so many aspects of Chinese life, most of them are directly or indirectly related to the precepts of Confucianism. Thus, the other-orientedness of Chinese was not only actually mentioned by several of the participants and detailed in the friendship elements of sharing, caring, and helping; it also transpired through its side effects. Thus, the warm, benevolent, and sympathetic nature of the Chinese students in this sample is said to be a by-product of collectivism, as is patience and a lower level of aggression, both remarked upon as lacking in Americans. That verbal communication plays a lesser role in Chinese culture was also mentioned by the participants. The most important feature of collectivism, however, is strong group cohesiveness, which satisfies inclusion needs and leads to low affiliativeness. Thus, all of the participants in this study, even though they proclaimed not being too involved in the Chinese student organization, had many conational friends on campus. Participants stated that Chinese welcome parties, get-togethers, and shared holiday celebrations made it easy to keep in touch and make friends with fellow Chinese. Except for Shih-Ming (who was very content) and in part Chia-Ling (who was content but self-admittedly avoided more extensive involvement to alleviate her reentry in Taiwan), they also mentioned that if they had a problem, they would seek help from their Chinese friends first. Because of this Chinese support group and the temporariness of their sojourn, they did not perceive the lack of American friends as intolerable.

The second maxim of Confucianism, the hierarchical social structure, and related to it authoritarianism and filial piety, was also touched upon by participant comments. Thus, repeated references were made to the closeness and supportiveness within the family and the fact that sharing of family matters is sometimes excluded even from the closest friendships.

Possibly most effectual in this study, however, was the third precept of Confucianism, the adherence to role requirements, social norms, and proper conduct. It is the culture clash in this category that threw Chiu-Mei off balance and caused Hsiu-Hui to become cautious and even reticent when interacting with Americans. Shih-Ming's unfortunate money transaction might also be grouped here, even though he managed to retain his optimism and good spirit despite the experience. In all of these cases, the Taiwanese students expected certain behaviors and trusted in the support and integrity of the Americans involved.

Especially in Chiu-Mei's case, their advisor's deviation from these role expectations effected such a profound loss of face as to overshadow years of her sojourn. This sensitivity and need for face protection is also illustrated by an occurrence that Hsiu-Hui related. When she asked her pastor friend whether she could borrow a certain trinket for a class presentation, he jokingly said "no," pretending that she had taken and not returned many things in his house. Hsiu-Hui did not understand the irony, got very upset, and unbeknownst to the pastor "cried for many days" until the matter was clarified. It comes as no surprise that with this absolute faith in others' support and integrity, Chinese give the impression of easily being taken advantage of by less virtuous contemporaries.

While the above experience and observations confirmed findings in the research literature, two aspects were contradicted. Thus, research purports that the self-disclosure of deep feelings is reserved for the family whereas participants in this study all reported profound levels of sharing in their close friendships, too. Research literature also paints the picture of taciturn, shy, and passive females. While the females in this study were maybe not as happy-go-lucky as the males, at least Chia-Ling and Hsiu-Hui appeared very outspoken, confident, and active in the pursuit of their goals. In addition, the participants did not feel bound in their activities (e.g., intercultural dating) by the approval or disapproval of the larger Taiwanese student community. With research literature reporting a trend towards increasingly individualistic, extraverted, and critical personalities, these deviations might well be a sign for recently occurring changes.

Chapter 9

Case Study Results

The data gathered in this study lend themselves to a discussion on two levels. Thus, in the following section, overall findings concerning the actual friendship experiences of the informants will be analyzed and contrasted with the status quo delineated in the existing literature. On a more theoretical level, the data will be related to the factors composing the friendship model introduced earlier.

Friendship Experiences

In the research literature concerning American friendship patterns and intercultural friendships between foreign students and Americans, two conflicting images emerge. For one, close American friendship intraculturally is in general depicted as featuring elements commonly attributed to close relationships across many cultures: Trust, honesty, loyalty, mutuality, generosity, warmth, supportiveness, and acceptance are mentioned as the most prominent ones. Publications for and about foreign sojourners, on the other hand, all warn that close friendships in the United States are less intense and short-lived, if they happen at all. In a sense, both images are reflected in the findings of this study, relating to and contradicting each other in a kaleidoscopic manner. Several focal points reveal themselves thereby.

Thus, many participants referred to the broad meaning of the term *friend* in the United States, mentioning that Americans consider someone a friend after what seems a shockingly brief interaction time. As Marlene put it: "For Americans, friendship is as soon as you know somebody, as soon as you know more than the subject of study, the name, and the address; then, you are friends." A little less sarcastically, Arnold states:

> Here it's very often that people call you a friend although they just know you for two weeks . . . . In Germany you are hardly able to call somebody a friend. You might even know him [her] for over a year, but if you don't have that special emotional relationship, you wouldn't call him [her] your friend.

The point of contention hereby is that friendships in the home cultures of the participants in general have a much longer incubation period during which intimacy and trust can develop. Thus, Kuo-Hsiang commented in reference to the constant flux of incoming and graduating students: "It's hard to be a good friend in just two years."

Some students conceded that the problem is merely linguistic and solved by matching the equivalent, more narrowly defined nomers of other cultures with the term *close friend* instead of just *friend*. Other participants opined that the predicament is caused by the devaluation of the concept in general, making American friendship the low-duration, low-obligation experience described in the literature which, in the eyes of some foreign sojourners, lacks sincerity and depth and almost desecrates the entity. Thus, Marlene supplied the example of an American acquaintance who "always talked about her best friend in Washington, her best friend in Los Angeles, her best friend in Athens, Georgia." While research literature points out that friendship definitions are highly subjective and intracultural accounts of close American relationships provide counterexamples for this verdict of superficialty, it cannot be merely brushed off as a figment of some culture-shocked or ethnocentric students' imagination. If for no other reason than being constantly mentioned, it constitutes a crossroad which divided at least the participants in this study into three distinct camps (see Figure 2). The measures hereby were intimacy needs and levels of

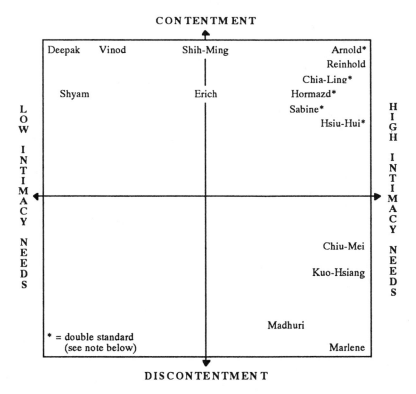

Figure 2. Relationship between levels of contentment and intimacy needs in intercultural friendships among study participants.

Note: Participants whose names are asterisked employed a double standard in evaluating American friendship patterns, characterizing their close American friends as atypical and higher than average in their capacity for intimacy.

contentment concerning close friendships with Americans as reported during the interview process.

Interestingly, only 4 of the 15 participants (Marlene, Madhuri, Kuo-Hsiang, and Chiu-Mei) place in the quadrant for high intimacy needs and a high level of discontentment. This is surprising since reports of prevailing foreign student complaints about the shallowness of American friendships and dissatisfaction with the number of close relationships lead to expectations of a much larger contingent in this field.

While only these four students had unfulfilling experiences, the vast majority expressed contentment. In direct contradiction to claims of superficialty, the larger number of students (Arnold, Reinhold, Chia-Ling, Hormazd, Sabine, and Hsiu-Hui) exhibited pronounced needs for intimacy and reported that their close American friends matched their ideals of sharing, caring, and reliability. It has to be noted, however, that five out of the six participants in this group employed a double standard in their descriptions of American friendship. Thus, they maintained that their relationships were atypical or nonaverage and deviated from the less compatible norm. In delineating this norm, familiar descriptors surfaced, and Americans in general were depicted mirroring the cautionary notes in the literature geared to foreign sojourners. Thus, the average American was characterized as merely fun-loving and activity-oriented, initially friendly but then closed, not interested in serious talks or sharing of personal matters, self-centered, volatile, and unreliable. It leaves to be resolved whether this discrepancy between actual positive experience and general negative definition reflects a tendency to automatically reiterate commonly held stereotypes and to consider deviants exceptions to the rule or whether the participants indeed sought out atypical and nonaverage Americans as their close friends. The question was not answered in the course of this study but most likely comprises both facets. Thus, it is notable that the five students with the double standard shared among each other half of the total number of listed American friends which, if numbers could speak, would support the notion of their having repeated stereotypes that are not reflected in reality. On the other hand, participants often mentioned that their close friends were more internationally interested, interculturally sensitive, and intellectual than other Americans--an observation in favor of the atypicality theory. Another controversial finding is that all the content students disproved research reports that the primary support network of foreign sojourners in the United States is that of conationals, with Americans frequently only serving as academic or professional contacts and other internationals fulfilling recreational needs. Most of the participants in this study maintained that their American friends are equal to their close home country or international friends in all functions of friendship. The only difference mentioned repeatedly was that the friendships at home had had more time to develop and were therefore more stable.

With two students (Shih-Ming and Erich) placing in the middle between low and high intimacy needs, the third camp of participants is composed of three students (Deepak, Vinod, and Shyam) with low needs for intimacy and a high level of contentment. What distinguishes this group, is a satisfaction with activity-oriented and often fleeting friendships and what seems a general absence of relational demands. In fact, in line with the supposition of self-disclosure as a key to close friendship formation, the question arises whether these participants' friendship experiences do not fall in the casual rather than close category--a notion supported by Deepak's inability to differentiate between the two descriptors. On a similar note, Deepak, Vinod, and even Erich could not supply an answer when asked how numbers of close and casual friends compared between cultures. Except for Kuo-Hsiang who claimed lack of knowledge about American culture, all other participants readily replied, with most of them declaring that Americans have more casual and fewer close friends than people in their cultures. (At an average, participants listed four to five close friendships per person in their home countries.) Only Hormazd and Chiu-Mei believed that the numbers were the same.

Noticeably, no participant placed in the quadrant for low intimacy needs and high levels of discontentment. It would be interesting to see whether this situation is reversed for activity-oriented sojourners in surroundings that stress intimate talk and sharing.

Summarizing these findings, the following picture emerges: While some of the students in this study fit the widely purported mold of the discontented foreign student lacking truly close friendships with Americans, most others have found satisfying relationships ranging from high to low levels of intimacy according to the individuals' needs. This constellation deviates from the image portrayed in the research literature and therefore calls for interpretation. Several viewpoints offer themselves hereby. Thus, it has to be kept in mind that the sample was self-selected and might, therefore, feature individuals unrepresentative in their propensity for the subject matter and their levels of contentment. In addition, all participants were graduate students, single, from a limited range of cultures, and fairly long-term residents in the United States, thus possibly further skewing results. However, the purpose of qualitative research is not generalizability and predictability but an authentic representation of the situation under study and the uncovering of meaningful and relevant categories. With this having been attempted in the grouping of the participants, some potential explanations for the unexpected diversity in friendship experiences are plausible.

Thus, it has to be noted that all the participants with low intimacy needs and high levels of contentment were male. If Shih-Ming and Erich are included in this group, its members come from all three cultures, possibly reflecting a global tendency of males--or at least somewhat Westernized males--to shy away from intimacy. This explanation would extend observations about American male and female friendship patterns earlier presented. On the other hand, the study also yielded results surprisingly equalizing in nature. Thus, even though cross-gender friendships are supposedly more acceptable in Germany than in the United States but less common in India and Taiwan, the occurrences of friendships between men and women in the sample were evenly spread across nationalities, with two participants from each culture reporting at least one close American friend across gender lines.

Beyond these gender considerations, differences in friendship personality type similar to the ones found in the United States intraculturally may account for some of the diversity. Thus, depending on where an individual is situated on the continuum from independent to acquisitive and discerning, he or she might not need intimate contact to be satisfied with the sojourn experience.

The gender and personality questions are but two possible explanations for the diverse findings of this study. More general but still related factors influencing the friendship experiences of the participants will be discussed in the next section and may shed more light also on this issue. The search for explanations and conclusions should not divert attention from the core of the findings, however, namely the fact that the participants were far more heterogeneous in their desires and friendships than research literature leads us to believe. With this being the case, there might be hope that the actual friendship experiences of foreign students on a broader scale might also not be as one-dimensional and bleak as commonly portrayed.

Friendship Model

The purpose of this study was to create foundational knowledge concerning intercultural friendship patterns; it was not to prove or disprove the elements of the friendship model that emerged from the research literature. Nevertheless, some of the data derived from this study illustrate the model by providing examples for factors influencing intercultural friendship, and it is under this premiss that they will be presented here. The study was not conducted with the model in mind and it, therefore, merely serves as an avenue for organizing and sharing information. Consequently, the following account is by no means comprehensive or meant to test the applicability of the model.

In the model, 12 key factors influencing intercultural friendship were identified: culture, personality, self-esteem, friendship elements, expectations, adjustment stage, cultural knowledge, communicative competence, external variables, proximity, U.S. elements, and chemistry. The first of these factors, culture, refers to mainly the deep cultural background of an individual. Deep culture, of course, is a vast concept with many possible points of departure for discussion. In this study, several focal points crystallized and will be summarized here. Thus, U.S. friendship patterns in general were described as low in obligation, duration, and context, and high in spread as purported in the literature. In line with Lewin's public and private layers, the initial friendliness of Americans but subsequent barrier preventing closeness was also mentioned repeatedly, not just by German participants. (As noted earlier, however, many participants employed a double standard and depicted their close American friends as different and not possess-ing the negative characteristics of the norm.) Despite the satisfying friendship experiences reported by the majority of the participants, differences in culture were perceived as separating by some. As Erich puts it: "I still feel that even though we are friends, we're from two different countries and two different backgrounds." The similarity of cultures thereby did not seem to play as big a role as maintained in the research literature. Thus, the Indian or Chinese participants did not perceive more distance in their close friendships than the Germans whose culture is supposedly closer to U.S. culture. The Chinese did, however, list more disturbing occurrences and misunderstandings that can be traced back to cultural differences. Thus, Chiu-Mei's disappointment concerning her aloof advisor and Shih-Ming's surprise at his Dutch-treat professor are effects of a culture clash between the individualistic United States and the rules of Confucianism, requiring proper conduct within the social hierarchy and the support and integrity connected with other-orientedness. The oftmentioned tendency of students from collectivistic cultures to band together was also noticeable as a trend in some of the Chinese students but not as pronounced as expected. The reason for this and other observed atypicalities might be that the unique interpersonal styles and individual identities of sojourners are not always representative of their cultural background and, in some cases, might actually lean more towards that of the contact culture. Indeed, the most marked predication emerging from this study is that expectations based on home country generalizations can often not be sustained and individuals should therefore not be labeled according to cultural origin.

Frequently, it is the personality of an individual that is more decisive in influencing intercultural friendship than his or her cultural background. Thus, most of the participants in this study seemed to be personal instead of cultural identifiers, going about their lives in an independent way and not taking refuge in groups with fellow nationals. Other personality traits surfacing repeatedly and greatly matching descriptions in the research literature were empathy and patience, flexibility and world-mindedness, a balanced and resilient temper, honesty and openness, and a relaxed attitude and good sense of humor. While a few of the participants (Sabine, Madhuri, and to an extent all Chinese females) appeared to be on the introverted end of the spectrum, the other students were markedly extraverted. Among introverted and extraverted participants alike, however, the consensus was that it is essential to go out and make an active effort in making friends with Americans.

Very closely related to personality is self-esteem. Except for Chiu-Mei, who seemed to suffer an identity crisis due to self-shock, the participants of this study appeared extremely confident and self-assured. Thus, self-esteem rarely emerged as an issue. Only Sabine and Hsiu-Hui remarked that they gave up easily in the pursuit of American contacts, but ascribed this tendency to their reserved nature rather than doubts in their capabilities. Interestingly, the line between introversion and weak self-esteem seems often blurred in the research literature. Thus, while extraversion is proclaimed as one of the elements facilitating friendship formation, the findings of this study suggest that self-esteem may override this principle. Most of the introverted participants seemed quite adept in forming friendships and content with their experiences, which can in all likelihood be ascribed to their evidently high levels of self-awareness and self-esteem. While lack of confidence was not a problem for the actual participants in this study, two of the Indian students mentioned that it often hinders some of their fellow nationals from reaching out and developing close American friendships. Thus, they claimed that many Indian sojourners band together not only out of fear of conational ostracization but also because they are too self-conscious about being different and too scared of ridicule--a fact exacerbated by feelings of inferiority due to India's third-world status. As mentioned in the research literature, a combination of high cultural identification, low self-esteem, and low accorded national status is least conducive to establishing close host culture relationships.

Elements concerning the actual dynamics of friendships include differing friendship styles, homophily, and developmental stages. While differences in friendship-related personality types are mentioned in the intracultural literature (e.g., independent, discerning, and acquisitive styles), intercultural research has not delved into this issue. Yet, findings in this study suggest that expectations concerning friendship range from a pure activity-orientation to the most intimate sharing and vary, disrespective of culture, from individual to individual, with the only trend being a lower need for intimacy in some males. Traditional limitations on cross-gender friendships could also not be confirmed in this study; no pattern emerged, but the tendency was towards liberal practices, with students from all cultures reporting close American friends across gender lines. The second of the friendship elements mentioned above, homophily, got a similarly mixed reception. Thus, while a few of the participants maintained that shared interests can create a welcome entrance into a relationship, most others disclaimed the importance of commonalities in this respect, only listing similarities in personality, attitudes, or values as decisive factors. Some participants even negated this stipulation, saying that the sole determiner of friendship is a caring interest and trust in each other. It has to be noted, however, that even though they were not recognized as such, many of the participants' relationships did contain additional aspects of homophily, preeminently an international orientation and comparable levels of intellectuality. The only claim found in the research literature concerning friendship elements mirrored in this study was that cultural and sociological data play a role mainly during the orientation and exploratory affective stage of friendship formation. Once close relationships are established, interactions have a personalistic focus, with each person treated uniquely and cultural stereotypes broken down. Marlene describes this process, referring to her Singaporean friend:

> We just had different expectations, different attitudes in the beginning, but at the end we were so close that we didn't have to talk about it . . . . After we erased all prejudices, that we thought the other person has to be different, after we erased that by talking, we just understood each other.

While expectations can be directed towards one particular person as in the quote above, they also can refer to the sojourn as a whole and as such represent another key factor influencing intercultural friendship formation. A major division thereby occurs between task-oriented students focusing on degree work or professional training and cross-cultural seekers with an adaptive motivation who strive for self-development through interaction with host country nationals. While task-orientation usually has a negative effect on the number and nature of intercultural friendships, however, it does not necessarily cause dissatisfaction with relationships. As Deepak, Vinod, and Shyam show, a task-orientation in combination with low intimacy needs can leave students quite content with their social life. Another favorable factor in this respect is, of course, a limited sojourn length and an existing conational support group. As some of the Indian and Chinese participants remarked, the temporariness of their stay and the presence of fellow national friends makes the lack of American contacts quite endurable. It is only when one plans to remain longer and possibly enter the world of work, that being accepted in U.S. society becomes more of a priority. Unfortunately, the situation is at times not as uncomplicated for cross-cultural seekers. Thus, a person with adaptive motivation will be quite frustrated by the absence of American friends, especially when respective hopes were high before the sojourn. It is these students that Reinhold addresses when he says: "Don't avoid parties . . . take every opportunity. If you're just concerned about your studies, you can't make American friends." Hormazd adds the advice, however, to "just get what you can get" and not to expect too much.

While culture, personality, self-esteem, friendship elements, and expectations constitute predispositions in the process of intercultural friendship formation, adjustment stages, cultural knowledge, communicative competence, and external variables have their effect mainly during the actual sojourn. The first of these factors, adjustment stages, includes the development of intercultural sensitivity of an individual in general and the various stages of culture shock. While the latter concept is not applicable to the participants in this study since all had been in the United States for a time period beyond its reaches, several indicators concerning intercultural sensitivity can be related to the friendship focus at hand and deserve mentioning. Thus, Marlene exhibits signs of the defense stage, namely recognizing cultural differences, evaluating them negatively, and considering her background superior. It comes to no surprise that she has no close American friends and seems most discontent with her experience. Deepak, Vinod, and Shyam appear to be in a stage of minimization, seeing practically no differences between friendship in India and the United States and exhibiting a generally indiscriminating attitude. Most progressed on the continuum from ethnocentric to ethnorelative stages seem to be Reinhold and Shih-Ming, showing signs of acceptance and even adaptation. They view host culture ways as viable alternatives in organizing the world, exhibit empathy, and avail themselves in parts of a bicultural repertoire. In respect to the five students who were satisfied with their actual friends but employed a double standard concerning American friendship patterns in general, an interesting situation arises. Thus, even though their level of contentment is high, they have not reached the ethnorelative end of the spectrum yet; exempting positive manifestations or people from an otherwise negative norm is still thought an ethnocentric stage of development.

A precondition for acceptance and adaptation is cultural knowledge; i.e., familiarity with the elements of deep culture and ease in using them in daily life. Many of the points of contention mentioned by the participants have their origin in a lack of cultural knowledge. Thus, the misunderstandings surrounding the category width of the term *friend*, the initial friendliness and perceived subsequent barrier to closeness, or the role expectations concerning Chiu-Mei's advisor and Shih-Ming's professor fall under this category and could have been prevented or at least ameliorated had the participants possessed in-depth knowledge of these phenomena, including their hidden reasons and possible explanations. Unfortunately, comprehensive culture-specific information is still rare and many intercultural sojourners, in the spirit of true adventurers, are faced with having to gain this knowledge in sink-or-swim fashion.

The factor with maybe the most far-reaching influence on intercultural friendship formation is communicative competence. As Vinod puts it: "Language has a lot to do with it . . . . Indians and other foreign students who have problems with the language tend to stay in a smaller group with their own people." Of course, language proficiency is only one part of communicative competence which also includes a myriad of other communication skills, desirable personal attributes, and culture-specific and culture-general knowledge related to communication. Obviously, the short duration and artificialty of the interview process did not allow for an in-depth evaluation of the participants' communicative competence. From what could be observed, however, at least the students' language skills per se were excellent. Only the Chinese showed moderate deficiencies and repeatedly intimated that communicating with their Chinese friends was much easier comparatively, especially when exploring subjects on a deeper level. Concerning culture-specific details, some other differences emerged. Thus, the German in this study preferred interaction featuring analysis, criticism, and seriousness of content and form, noticing that Americans in general communicate on a much lighter plain. Some of the students from Taiwan, on the other hand, pointed out that Americans were more verbal and less intuitive than the Chinese conforming the often mentioned dichotomy between individualistic, low-context and collectivistic, high-context cultures. Even though these differences were known to the participants, most of them seemed to consider their style preferable and did not move to adjust to American practices. The hypothesis offers itself that communication patterns, encoding the core of a culture and expressing so much one's identity, are the toughest entity to duplicate on the road to biculturalism.

Beside adjustment stages, cultural knowledge, and communicative competence some minor external variables are said to influence intercultural friendship formation. These are previous transition experience, socioeconomic status, level of education, area of studies, source of financial support for the sojourn, urban or rural background, and gender. Of these variables, only a few received notice in the course of the study and the results concerning these few were inconclusive or did not confirm suggested tendencies. Thus, while about half the participants had traveled extensively prior to their U.S. sojourn, it was not clear whether these excursions constituted actual transition experiences. If they did no pattern emerged concerning friendship formation; the respective students were spread fairly evenly across the different levels of contentment. The element of educational level played a role in this study in that all participants and their friends were university educated. However, since no comparison with other population groups were undertaken, the stipulation that higher levels of education facilitate friendship formation cannot be evaluated. Concerning the field studies, it is noticeable that most of the students with high intimacy needs and high levels of contentment had a humanistic orientation and all students with low intimacy needs and high levels of contentment were in the sciences. Since all of the students in the latter group were also male (which is the only gender-related trend in this study) and counterexamples existed for the former tendency, the findings signify an inclination but do not provide clear support for the research claim that humanities majors supply a more fertile ground for friendship formation than science majors. Finally, the proposition that an urban background is a favorable precondition could also not be confirmed, with only two participants being from rural areas and both being successful and content concerning their close American friendships.

Proximity to host nationals and contact frequency at the beginning stages of close relationships are considered essential ingredients in friendship formation. Research literature purports that lodging with or in the vicinity of Americans and regular participation in community activities are advisable means to ensure this proximity and contact frequency. In respect to the participants in this study, 4 out of the 28 close Americans friends listed were found due to leisure time activities or through introductions by common acquaintances, and 8 friendships originated in housing arrangements.   The vast majority of close American relationships, however, owed their existence to the proximity and contact frequency afforded by the participants' studies. Thus, 15 friendships involved classmates, labmates, and officemates, supporting some of the students' claims that their studies do not leave much time for other activities. Interestingly, all friendships were formed independently, without the guidance of programs geared to foreign students. Thus, only one participant, Madhuri, wished for a larger number of community friend referrals and the involvement of more Americans in international events on campus. Reflecting this trend towards autonomy among most of the students in this study, the general consensus was that individuals are responsible for creating proximity and contact frequency themselves by not excluding Americans from their social life and instead reaching out actively and persevering in the pursuit of friendships.

Whereas all of the abovementioned key factors effecting intercultural friendship formation can to some extend be controlled by the foreign students, the last two categories escape such influence. Thus, U.S. elements comprise American idiosyncracies facing the foreign student that cannot be manipulated and leave the sojourner in a reactive mode. Concerning this study, the participants' characterizations of Americans can be divided into three tiers. For one, students mentioned positive traits such as independence, friendliness, and informality. One student, Arnold, also remarked that Germans, in contrast to some less accepting European countries, were surprisingly well-received in the United

States. In the same vein, Reinhold states that Americans in general "welcome people with open arms." On a more negative note, the participants reverberated oftmentioned complaints listed in the research literature and thus described Americans as closed to intimate contact, too transient to establish long-lasting friendships, self-centered, lacking seriousness, indifferent to foreign students, often having an air of superiority, being simplistic and unaware of world affairs, and insensitive concerning language problems of sojourners. An additional feature not mentioned in the research literature but repeatedly pointed out by the participants was that Americans often lacked sincerity and were unreliable. The third tier concerning U.S. elements features the statements of the students who employed a double standard in depicting American friendship patterns, listing predominantly negative attributes in general but describing their close friends in glowing terms. Thus, these American friends were characterized as caring, considerate and helpful, intellectual with travel experiences and international interests, willing to listen, sensitive concerning language and culture gaps, sincere, and dependable when it came to keeping promises. Most importantly, however, they treated their foreign friends "in an equal manner" and "like a regular person, not a foreigner." Again, the reasons for the discrepancy between general definition and actual friendship experience were not explored. Whatever the explanation, however, the picture of desirable traits in host nationals emerges with clarity and may serve to guide the actions of American friends and possibly even host nationals on a global scale.

Chemistry, the last and most elusive factor influencing intercultural friendship formation, was only twice mentioned in the research literature and received even scarcer attention from the participants in this study. Thus, only Hormazd recognized the existence of a supernatural bond between individuals, predetermined through reincarnation. This is in correspondence with the Chinese concept of *yuan* which is the subject of the single extensive treatment of the phenomenon in the literature and also describes the affinity between individuals caused by past-life experiences. As is evident, this final decisive force in friendship formation has been the least investigated of all and awaits further exploration and enlightenment.

Chapter 10

Implementations

The focus of this study was to provide descriptive, foundational knowledge for a newly evolving area of research: intercultural friendship. In line with this objective, a qualitative research design was chosen to supply perspective, empirical assessment, and context-bound information, and to create a critical data experience base. Specifically, the study was to afford an in-depth view of the actual intercultural friendship experiences of individual foreign students in the United States, an exploration of culture-specific trends concerning the national background of the informants (Germany, India, and Taiwan), a comparison of the findings with the status quo delineated in the research literature, and an application of the data to a friendship model detailing factors influencing intercultural friendship formation.

The necessity for dense description at the exploratory stage of a subject is well-documented in the literature, but receives an especially urgent recommendation from Roland (1986, p. 111):

> International migration increasingly produces complex cross-cultural contexts and interactions . . . . At the macro-level we may think of it as a global society. But on closer inspection . . . it is made up of many emerging institutions, goups, networks, families, friendships. These can be identified, located, and documented. It would repay much effort to learn more about what forms these emergent collectivities take, who participates, why they fail and how they succeed, and what "success" means to their members.

Research at times seems to shortcut this qualitative data collection process and provides culture comparisons that lack extensive foundational knowledge and therefore have to remain largely tentative (Poortinga & Malpass, 1986, p. 19). While incomprehensive methods and hastily drawn conclusions lurk on one end of the spectrum, the meticulous researcher is faced with another danger. Thus, in-depth decriptions of experiences often lead to a segmentation of "knowledge and human identity into meaningless fragments" (Saral, 1979, p. 78). The focus of foundational research, however, is not necessarily on "developing catalogues of habit patterns of various cultures, but on facilitating a process, in-culture self-knowledge, which is a necessary prerequisite for any effective communication" (Saral, 1979, p. 79). This condition can only be promoted if the intricacies of human personalities, the complex interconnections between people, and the true nature of authentic interaction are not lost to fragmentation.

In keeping with this spirit, the following holistic image of intercultural friendship emerged from the findings of this study. While some culture-specific and some culture-general patterns suggested in the research literature outlined themselves sporadically, cultural background and universal predictors in general proved much less significant than expected. Thus, the single-most important element manifesting itself was the individuality of each participant. Whereas personalities are obviously shaped and changed by one's cultural background, it has to be noted that each culture produces many variants depending on an individual's parents, community, occupation, and all other influences occurring during formative years and beyond (Singh, Huang, & Thompson, 1962, p. 123). In addition to these external elements, however, personalities also comprise internal factors independent of cultural affiliation. It is these factors that were clearly pronounced in the informants of this study. Thus, all participants were not cultural but personal identifiers and seemed to have a high degree of self-awareness and confidence.

Maybe because of their individuality, many of the propositions about foreign students and intercultural friendship offered in the research literature could not be confirmed or were contradicted. Most importantly, claims of sojourner dissatisfaction with close friendships in theUnited States were confuted. Thus, the majority of the participants reported contentment and, concerning their close friends, did not share the oftenmentioned complaints about Americans being superficial, distant, and noncommittal. It has to be noted that some informants employed a double standard and did attribute these undesirable traits to Americans in general, excluding their friends. Whether this double standard is not detected in quantitative studies and thus has lead to the dissemination of only the bleak image was not explored in this study and needs to be investigated in future research. If a faulty assumption exists, however, it would also explain the dichotomy between the generally positive portrayal of American friendship in intracultural publications contrary to the dismal picture provided concerning the intercultural friendship experiences of foreign students.

While the tendency of all informants towards individualistic identities constituted a common denominator in this study, it also is the cause for the unpredicted diversity among the group. Related to friendship formation, three major factors emerged hereby. For one, the students in this study were heterogeneous concerning the meaning and expectations they assigned to the concept of close friendships. Similar to American informants in intracultural studies, they comprised a range of personality types with an activity-orientation and low needs for intimacy on one extreme and a desire for intimate talk and self-disclosure on the other. They also showed a mixture of task- and adaptive motivation, but proved that the former does not necessarily lead to a dissatisfying social life. Especially when task-orientation is coupled with a preferrence for activities and low needs for intimacy, it can produce very high contentment. The third factor marked by diversity concerns adjustment stages. By influencing attitudes towards host nationals, adjustment stages also effect friendship experiences.

To summarize, the study showed that in every individual a highly complicated interplay of characteristics, motivations, and impulses is at work. While light can be shed on these elements, each person as a whole contains them in such countless nuances and interwoven combinations that dissections and generalizations are largely precluded. A holistic interpretation of individual friendship experiences takes this almost magical configuration into account and seems, therefore, most appropriate for describing the reality of intercultural friendship.

Suggestions for Future Research

It is in the nature of a descriptive, foundational investigation to uncover areas in need of attention and thus provide recommendations for more directed explorations. In this study, a myriad of research ideas surfaced leading to the following questions which may serve to guide future research:

1.   What are the reasons for the abovementioned dichotomy between the positive descriptions of actual friendship experiences in both the intracultural literature and this study on one hand and the generally negative portrayal in intercultural publications?

2.   How comprehensive and applicable is the presented friendship model? In answering this question, special attention should be paid to areas exhibiting an inconclusiveness and contradiction between the research literature and the findings of this study.

   a. More culture-specific information about   friendship patterns is needed. This information should delineate the importance of friendship in a specific culture, its rank within the social hierarchy, and the meanings and expectations assigned to it. It should also include an analysis of deep structures and causality to afford psychological and historical explanations of the uncovered phenomena and thus promote empathy and aid sojourners' understanding.

   b. The existence of various personality types concerning friendship formation within cultures needs to be further investigated.

   c. Examinations are in line concerning the role of homophily as a multifaceted factor versus the single commonality of an international perspective. The question arises hereby whether a shared international orientation does not carry the exclusive significance reported by some informants only during the ethnocentric adjustment stages of sojourners and is replaced by more general aspects of homophily in accepting or adapted individuals. This hypothesis would be supported by the argument that the main function of homophily is validation of self- and role identities and that during early adjustment stages the self-consciousness of being different may eclipse other facets of the sojourner's identity.

d. Issues of communicative competence specifically related to friendship formation and development need to be explored and strategies for their integration into foreign student orientation or language classes developed.

e. The role of external variables, such as previous transition experience, field of studies, and demographic background, requires clarification.

3. What can the involved third parties (e.g., foreign student personnel, immigration workers, intercultural trainers, foreign language educators) do to support sojourners in their quest for close friends? As Y. Y. Kim (1991, p. 268) states: "Individuals who hope to carry out effective intercultural interactions must be equipped with a set of abilities to be able to understand and deal with the dynamics of culture difference, intergroup posture, and the inevitable stress experience." How can the cultural knowledge and self-esteem necessary in this process be imparted to the sojourner and what other skills need to be acquired? Specifically, what is the role of the foreign language teacher in preparing students for the intercultural experience? How can a narrow language-skills perspective be expanded to include the other elements of communicative competence? And how can cultural knowledge be effectively incorporated into such a curriculum?

4. Which actions would facilitate a more favorable reception of foreigners and prepare a fertile ground for friendship formation on part of the host culture?

5. How do people select their friends; do active or passive methods prevail? What strategies do host nationals employ in the pursuit of friendships? Are sojourners aware of these strategies and do they replicate them? What can be done to increase not only contact per se but to make it meaningful and intimate?

6. What constitutes chemistry and which role does it play in friendship formation and development?

7. If, as this study shows, some foreign students are quite able to form intercultural friendships and are satisfied with the experience, how can help be directed towards sojourners who are

not as successful? What are the characteristics of the discontented students? How many desire close involvement and are willing to put forth an effort to change their situation? What are the problem areas and which skills are necessary for their eradication (e.g., how can collectivistically oriented people gain the self-reliance needed to function in an individualistic society)?

8.   What is the survival rate of friendships formed between foreign students and host nationals? How does duration compare intra- and interculturally for specific individuals? And what effects does a person's sojourn experience have on his or her friendships in the home country?

9.   Are there global tendencies in the roles and manifestations of friendship? It has been purported that social networks and communities are dissolving worldwide (Maybury-Lewis, 1992). While this trend may allow for greater creativity and individual expression, it also is said to be responsible for an increase in personal pain, social stress, isolation, and alienation. How does it influence intercultural friendship? Which functions would intercultural relationships fulfill in such an individualistic world?

These and no doubt countless other questions await examination in the future. Considering the relevance of global understanding and a peaceful coexistence of the world's cultures on one hand and the perfect suitability of friendship to foster the necessary awareness and promote precious bonds on the other, the problems listed seem pressing and requiring immediate solutions. While the task might appear overwhelming, however, it has to be kept in mind that in the meantime intercultural friendships are formed and do prosper worldwide. And if the findings of this study are any indication, at least some sojourners are intuitively or consciously quite adept in the process. It is left to future researchers to uncover this yet hidden knowledge and pass it on to the rest of our global village.

Appendices

Appendix A

Preliminary Questionnaire

Name:_____

Street:_____

City: _____ State: _____ Zip Code:_____

Phone: (day)_____ (evening) _____

Best time to call: _____

Check or fill in appropriate answers.

1. Sex: Male _____ Female _____
2. Age: _____
3. Marital Status:
    Never married _____ Divorced _____ Widowed _____
4. Graduate Student Status:
    1st year _____ 2nd year _____ 3rd year _____
    4th year _____ 5th year or more _____
5. Where did you get your undergraduate degree?

    _____
6. Are you also employed? Yes _____ No _____
7. If so, where?
    Assistantship _____ Job on campus _____
    Job off campus _____ Other _____
8. How long have you been in the U.S.?
    Years _____ Months _____
9. How much longer will your studies in the U.S. take?
    Years _____ Months _____

10. After finishing your studies in the U.S., what would you prefer to do?
    Stay in the U.S. _____ (years _____ forever _____)
    Return home _____ (years _____ forever _____)
    Go to a third country _____ (years _____ forever _____)
11. Is this your first visit to the U.S.? Yes _____ No _____
12. If answered no, how many years and/or months were you in the U.S. on previous visits? Years _____ Months _____
13. Have you other prior international experience (travel, studies etc.)? Yes _____ No _____
14. If so, describe briefly: _____
    _____
15. What is your major field of study? _____
16. What is your home country? _____
17. What is your home town? _____
18. How would you describe your home region?
    Urban _____ Rural _____ In between _____
19. In which part of the country is your home town?
    _____
20. Do you identify with a special cultural group in your home country? Examples for special cultural groups in the U.S. would be African-American, Hispanics, and American Indians (racial); Southerners, New Englanders (regional)? Yes _____ No _____
21. If so, what is the group? _____
22. Do you practice a religion? Yes _____ No _____
23. If so, which? _____
24. What is your father's occupation? _____
25. What is your mother's occupation? _____
26. Where do you currently live?
    University-owned residence hall _____
    Off-campus housing (other than with relative) _____
    With relative _____
27. Do you have roommates? Yes _____ No _____

28. If so, indicate the background and number of your roommates:
American _____ From your own country _____
From another country _____
29. Do you have relatives in the Athens area? Yes _____ No _____
30. If so, how often do you visit them? _____
31. Since coming to the U.S., have you made return trips to
your home country? Yes _____ No _____
32. If so, how many years, months, or weeks did you stay in
your home country?
Years _____ Months _____ Weeks _____
Years _____ Months _____ Weeks _____
Years _____ Months _____ Weeks _____
33. At this university, there are a number of associations for students
from abroad. Do you belong to one of these associations?
Yes _____ No _____
34. If so, which? _____
35. How long have you been a member of this association?
_____

36. In an average week, approximately how many hours do you spend
in activities of the student association?
_____

37. In an average week, approximately how many hours of your free
time do you spend with Americans_____
Persons from your country _____
Persons from other countries _____
38. Of your close friends in Athens, how many are
Americans _____ (students _____ non-students _____)
Persons from your country _____
(students _____ non-students _____)
Persons from other countries _____
(students _____ non-students _____)

39. Which are your areas of frequent and/or regular contact with Americans?

Studies _____ Workplace _____ Housing _____
General leisure _____ Outings _____ Sports _____
Discussions _____ Social activities _____
Artistic activities _____ Political activities _____
Religious activities _____ Holidays _____
Close friends _____ Other (explain) _____

40. Are your contacts with Americans as frequent as you wish?
Yes _____ No _____

41. If no, in which areas would you like more contact?

Studies _____ Workplace _____ Housing _____
General leisure _____ Outings _____ Sports _____
Discussions _____ Social activities _____
Artistic activities _____ Political activities _____
Religious activities _____ Holidays _____
Close friends _____ Other (explain) _____

42. If in need of information or assistance, where do you get it? If you go to more than one source, check each source you use.
(Americans = 1, persons from your home country = 2, persons from another foreign country = 3, publications = 4, other sources = 5)

	1	2	3	4	5
Questions about which courses to take, and which professors are recommended					
How best to prepare for courses					
How to find your way around the city					
Questions about American customs					
Questions concerning where to buy items					
Information on leisure time activities					

43. How wouldyou describe the reaction of most Americans to you?
    Very favorable _____ Moderately favorable _____
    Unfavorable _____
44. How do you rate your knowledge about American culture
    before coming to the U.S.?
    Very good _____ Good _____ Fair _____
    Poor _____Very poor _____
45. How do you rate your knowledge about American culture
    now?
    Very good _____ Good _____ Fair _____
    Poor _____Very poor _____
46. Did you take part in an orientation program that made you familiar
    with aspects of American culture?
    Yes _____ No _____
47. If so, where did the program take place?
    Home country _____ U.S. _____ Other country _____
48. How long was the program?
    1-2 hours _____ 3-4 hours _____ 1 day _____
    2-3 days _____ 4-5 days _____ Other _____
49. What is/are your native language/s?
    _____
50. How many years of English have you had in your home country?
    _____
51. How do you rate your English ability?
    Very good _____ Good _____ Fair _____ Poor _____
    Very poor _____
52. Approximately what percentage of your daily language use falls
    to English _____ % Native language _____ % Other _____ %

53.   How satisfied are you with the following areas? (very = 1,
      fairly =2, tolerably =3, minimally = 4, not at all = 5)

	1	2	3	4	5
Studies at University of Georgia					
Housing					
Social life					
Stay in U.S. in general					

Additional Comments:

Appendix B

Interview Guide

Introduction

1. Ideally speaking, what is a friend in your culture?
2. Do you personally share this definition or is your concept of friendship different?
3. How many close and casual friends does the average person in your culture have?
4. What do you think is the American definition of friendship?
5. How many close and casual friends does, in your estimation, the average person in the U.S. have?
6. Looking back at your stay in the U.S. and including the present, who are the persons you consider to be close friends?

Specific Information About Each Friend Mentioned

7. How old were you?
8. How old was your friend?
9. Where were you living?
10. Where did you meet this person?
11. Was there a particular occurrence that made this person a friend rather than an acquaintance?
12. Why do/did you consider this person your friend? (qualities, activities etc.)
13. What do/did you do with this friend?
14. What do/did you talk about?

15. Do you still consider this person to be a friend? Why or why not? (How was the friendship terminated?)
16. When did you last have contact with this person?
17. Have your feelings about this person changed over the years?
18. Did you ever feel that you couldn't do something for this person that she or he wanted you to do? Vice versa? (Was the conflict only between friends or were spouses and families involved?)
19. Have you ever felt uncomfortable in a situation in which your friend did something you disapproved of?
20. Is there something that you don't/didn't understand in your friend, that puzzles/puzzled you? What is/was your reaction?
21. How do/did you and your friend compare concerning political views, taste in music and movies etc.?
22. Are/were you friends with this person at the same time you are/were friends with another person?
23. How content are you with your friendship? What would you describe as problem areas?
24. Looking back at your life in your home country, who are the persons you consider to be close friends?
    (Repeat questions 7 through 23 for each person mentioned.)

Comparison

25. In what ways are your friendships at home different from your friendships with Americans? (qualities, activities, verbal and nonverbal communication, conversation topics etc.)
26. If you have a personal problem, whom do you tell?
27. You said in the questionnaire that you had _____ close American friends? Are you satisfied with that number?
    Why don't you have (more) American friends?
28. What are the positive and negative consequences of making friends with Americans?
29. How is a fellow national regarded who has a lot American friends?

Cross-Gender Friendships

30. Have you ever been friends with someone of the other sex? Why or why not? How is/was this different from being friends with someone of the same gender?
31. Is there a difference between cross-gender friendships in your culture and the U.S.?

Ex-Friends

32. Is there anyone who was a friend of yours at one time who is no longer a friend? What happened? (active/ passive split)

General Questions About Friendships

33. Have your friendships been different at different stages of your life? (e.g. Are friends you've made recently different from earlier friends?)
34. Why do you think you have maintained friendships with some people and not with others?
35. Thinking back over all your friends, who is or was your best friend? Why is/was this person special?
36. Do you consider spouses or other relatives to be friends, or do you think of friends and relatives differently?
37. If you were asked to give advice to a fellow national about how to make a friend in the U.S., what would your advice be?
38. Who was the last friend that you made? Do you think of your new friends differently from the friends you made earlier in your life?
39. Have there been times when you had to choose between two friends? Between your family and a friend?
40. How often do you feel lonely or homesick?
41. Have there been periods in your life when you felt that you had no friends? When friends mattered more or less than other times?

Appendix C

Methodology

Research Design

The research design is a qualitative survey in the form of a multiple case study involving a questionnaire and one long interview. Participants were volunteers from a pool of foreign students from three different countries.

Because not much groundwork has been laid in the field of intercultural friendship, the objective was to generate foundational information and to advance the knowledge base in the field rather than to prove or disprove hypotheses. A qualitative design was chosen to match this objective.

The process of exploring matter and uncovering meaningful and relevant categories has to precede the construction and subsequent testing of theory in undeveloped areas of research (Glaser & Strauss, 1967, pp. 1-18; Strauss, 1987, p. 6). Thus, at the foundation stage of theory building, the focus must not be on the experimental manipulation of one or two variables, but on extensive and holistic observation and collection of material (Barnlund, 1989, p. xvi; Howell, 1979, pp. 25-26). The dense description of case studies provides the tools necessary for this process and is thus eminently suited for discovering, or grounding, theory (Glaser & Strauss, 1967, p. 3). Elaborating on this premiss, Merriam (1988, p. xiii) states that case studies are also the best approach for understanding phenomena which call for improvement in practice. As Patton (1985, p. 1) states:

162   Appendices

This understanding is an end in itself, so that it is not attempting to predict what may happen in the future necessarily, but to understand the nature of that setting--what it means for participants to be in that setting, what their lives are like, what's going on for them, what their meanings are, what the world looks like in that particular setting and in the analysis to be able to communicate that faithfully to others who are interested in that setting.

Providing an in-depth documentation of individuals and their friendship experiences, this multiple case study tries to describe the overall quality of contact rather than its distinct variables and thus seeks to supply insights into a phenomenon that might lead to answers and solutions in the future.

The conceptual framework thereby is a cultural identity perspective; i.e., national affiliation is used to organize the data and identify categories. The underlying emic approach, focusing on specific cultures, was supplemented with etic procedures, attempting a broader view and the comparison of behavior across cultures (Jones, 1979, p. 57).

Role of Researcher

As a native German, a foreign student at the University of Georgia between 1980 and 1988, and an English as a Second Language instructor at the university from 1988 to 1994, I was very close to the subject at hand. The advantages of this involvement are a first-hand knowledge of many of the problems and joys inherent in intercultural friendship, and a sense of camaraderie between the participants and me. My not being American presumably also contributed to a greater sense of ease and openness among the participants when it came to sharing negative experiences. Disadvantages include a possible loss of perspective and bias toward patterns of friendship familiar to me. I controlled these risks by translating personal thoughts into more theoretical considerations, sharing my field notes with outside readers, and firmly adhering to the research questions (Miles & Huberman, 1984, p. 234).

It has to be noted here that the subjectivity of the researcher is a given, the experiential background of the observer even necessary in qualitative research. Experiential data, thereby, are notions drawn from the researcher's own personal, research, and literature-reading experience (Strauss, 1987, pp. 10-11). Thus, ethnographic description is always a translation, involving subjectivity and the amalgamated character of the single researcher's description and interpretation of multiple realities (Spradley, 1979, pp. 70-72). It is these realities of the informants, however, that also lend reliability to qualitative research. Thus, if care is taken to document their existence as described by the informants themselves, the translation effect can be minimized (Bogdan & Biklen, 1982, p. 30). Further consistency is provided if either single or multiple researchers are involved in all the steps to complete the project. It has to be noted that the involvement of several researchers is one technique of triangulation (i.e., using multiple sources and methods) and, therefore, good practice in qualitative research (Denzin, 1978, pp. 291-307). If only a single investigator is conducting a study, protection against errors should be ensured by peer examination (Miles & Huberman, 1984, p. 234). In the case of this study, all aspects--distributing and evaluating the preliminary questionnaire, conducting the interview, and analyzing the results--were carried out exclusively by me. As mentioned above, findings were shared with outside readers and comments were encouraged.

Data Analysis

After transcribing the interview tapes, the generated written data, together with the questionnaire results, were analyzed by qualitative data analysis techniques (Bogdan & Biklen, 1982; Glaser & Strauss, 1967; Goetz & LeCompte, 1984; Miles & Huberman, 1984; Strauss, 1987). With the goal of developing grounded theory, the guiding framework, thereby, was the constant comparative method, which consists of immersing oneself in the data to discover important themes, comparing incidents to emerging categories, integrating categories and their properties, reducing and customizing data analysis to solidify theories, and formulating the theories (Glaser & Strauss, 1967, pp. 105-113). Specific techniques used in the process were comprised of triangulation (i.e., using multiple sources and methods), coding (i.e., marking data according to categories or relationships), writing analytic memos (i.e., keeping track of coding results by recording emerging hypotheses and propositions), and creating integrative diagrams (i.e., visual devices for displaying surfacing information and relationships).

These techniques permitted examining small details while at the same time looking for the larger picture. They also lend process rigor to the study and controlled biases, thus strengthening reliability and validity of the findings. It has to be kept in mind that in qualitative research reliability is internal, not external. Thus, qualitative investigators are concerned with the comprehensiveness of their data, striving for a fit between what is recorded and what actually occurs rather than precise replicability and consistency across different observations (Bogdan & Biklen, 1982, p. 44; Goetz & LeCompte, 1984, p. 210). Whereas reliability is concerned with replicability, validity addresses the accuracy of scientific findings (Goetz & LeCompte, 1984, p. 210). Again, validity in qualitative research is internal, attempting authentic representation of reality rather than generalizability which is the goal of external validity (Goetz & LeCompte, 1984, p. 21).

The rationale behind this focus on internal reliability and validity is that "reality is holistic, multidimensional and ever-changing; it is not a single, fixed, objective phenomenon waiting to be discovered, observed, and measured" (Merriam, 1988, p. 167). Thus, the qualitative researcher does not strive for predictability but to be true to the people under study and to represent the context adequately and in enough detail to show the sensibility of his or her conclusions (Merriam, 1988, p. 168). Transferred to this study, data were comprehensively described and analyzed in order to illuminate the meaning of intercultural friendship as experienced by the participants during the time and setting of the study. This is in hope that the findings will yield foundation materials on which more heuristically or phenomenologically oriented investigations can be built in the future.

Bibliography

Albert, R. S., & Brigante, T. R. (1962). The psychology of friendship relations: Social factors. *Journal of Social Psychology, 56,* 33-47.

Althen, G. (1983). *The handbook of foreign student advising.* Yarmouth, Maine: Intercultural Press.

Althen, G. (1988). *American ways: A guide for foreigners in the United States.* Yarmouth, Maine: Intercultural Press.

Alter, J., Klopf, D., & Cambra, R. (1980). *Data on the oral communication practices of the Chinese.* Paper presented at the annual meeting of the Communication Association of the Pacific, Kobe, Japan. (ERIC Document Reproduction Service No. ED 188 260).

Angell, D. (1986). Bengalis in the United States: Patterns of participation and identity. In R. H. Brown & G. V. Coelho (Eds.), *Studies in third world societies: Vol. 38. Tradition and transformation: Asian Indians in America* (pp. 95-114). Williamsburg, Virginia: Department of Anthropology, College of William and Mary.

Argyle, M., & Henderson, M. (1984). The rules of friendship. *Journal of Social and Personal Relationships, 1,* 211-237.

Aristotle. (1953). *The ethics of Aristotle* (J. A. K. Thomson, Trans.). Baltimore: Penguin Books.

Barnlund, D. C. (1979). Verbal self-disclosure: Topics, targets, depths. In E. C. Smith & L. F. Luce (Eds.), *Toward internationalism: Readings in cross-cultural communication* (pp. 83-101). Rowley, Massachusetts: Newbury House.

Barnlund, D. C. (1989). *Communicative styles of Japanese and Americans: Images and realities.* Belmont, California: Wadsworth Publishing Company.

166   Bibliography

Barraclough, G. (Ed.). (1982). *The Times concise atlas of world history*. Maplewood, New Jersey: Hammond.

Bell, R. R. (1981). *Worlds of friendship*. Beverly Hills: Sage Publications.

Bennett, M. J. (1986). A developmental approach to training for intercultural sensitivity. *International Journal of Intercultural Relations, 10*, 179-196.

Berman, J. J., Murphy-Berman, V., & Pachauri, A. (1988). Sex differences in friendship patterns in India and in the United States. *Basic and Applied Social Psychology, 9*, 61-71.

Berry, J. W. (1980). Acculturation as varieties of adaptation. In A. M. Padilla (Ed.), *Acculturation: Theory, models and some new findings* (pp. 9-25). Boulder, Colorado: Westview Press.

Bishop, D. H. (1971). Caste in India: Past and present. *Social Studies, 62*, 10-15.

Blieszner, R. & Adams, R. G. (1992). *Adult friendship*. Newbury Park, California: Sage.

Block, J. D. (1980). *Friendship*. New York: Macmillan.

Bochner, S., Hutnik, N., & Furnham, A. (1985). The friendship patterns of overseas and host students in an Oxford student residence. *Journal of Social Psychology, 125*, 689-694.

Bochner, S., McLeod, B. M., & Lin, A. (1977). Friendship patterns of overseas students: A functional model. *International Journal of Psychology, 12*, 277-294.

Bogdan, R. C., & Biklen, D. K. (1982). *Qualitative research for education: An introduction to theory and methods*. Boston: Allyn and Bacon.

Bond, M. H., & Wong, G. Y. Y. (1986). The social psychology of Chinese people. In M. H. Bond (Ed.), *The psychology of the Chinese people* (pp. 213-266). New York: Oxford University Press.

Breen, M. P. (1986, July). *Friction caused by intercultural "false friends." Case study: America and Australia*. Paper presented at the annual meeting of the Australian Communication Association, Canberra, Australia. (ERIC Document Reproduction Service No. ED 272 035)

Brigham Young University Kennedy Center Publications (1993b). *Culturgram: China.* (Available from Kennedy Center Publications, Brigham Young University, Provo, Utah 84602)

Brigham Young University Kennedy Center Publications (1993b). *Culturgram: India.* (Available from Kennedy Center Publications, Brigham Young University, Provo, Utah 84602)

Brigham Young University Kennedy Center Publications (1993c). *Culturgram: Taiwan.* (Available from Kennedy Center Publications, Brigham Young University, Provo, Utah 84602)

Brislin, R. W. (1989). Intercultural communication training. In M. K. Asante & W. B. Gudykunst (Eds.), *Handbook of international and intercultural communication* (pp. 441-457). Newbury Park, California: Sage.

Brown, H. D. (1986). Learning a second culture. In J. M. Valdes (Ed.), *Culture bound: Bridging the cultural gap in language teaching* (pp. 33-48). New York: Cambridge University Press.

Brown, R. H. (1986). Self and polity in India and the United States. In R. H. Brown & G. V. Coelho (Eds.), *Studies in third world societies: Vol. 38. Tradition and transformation: Asian Indians in America* (pp. 1-25). Williamsburg, Virginia: Department of Anthropology, College of William and Mary.

Butterfield, F. (1982). *China: Alive in the bitter sea.* New York: Times Books.

Chang, H. B. (1973). Attitudes of Chinese students in the United States. *Sociology and Social Research, 58,* 66-77.

Chang, H. C., & Holt, G. R. (1991). The concept of *yuan* and Chinese interpersonal relationships. In S. Ting-Toomey & F. Korzenny (Eds.). *Cross-cultural interpersonal communication* (pp. 28-57). Newbury Park, California: Sage.

Chatterjee, B. B. (1983). Training and preparation for research in intercultural relations in the Indian subcontinent. In D. Landis & R. W. Brislin (Eds.), *Handbook of intercultural training* (Vol. 3) (pp. 196-226). New York: Pergamon Press.

Chen, G. M. (1988, April). *Relationships of the dimensions of intercultural communication competence.* Paper presented at the annual meeting of the Eastern Communication Association. (ERIC Document Reproduction Service No. ED 297 381)

Coelho, G. V. (1986). Cross-cultural learning and   adaptation: Main
    themes of coping with environmental   change. In R. H. Brown & G. V.
    Coelho (Eds.), *Studies in   third world societies: Vol. 38. Tradition and
    transformation: Asian Indians in America* (pp. 181-192).
    Williamsburg, Virginia: Department of Anthropology, College of
    William and Mary.

Cohen, Y. A. (1961a). Food and its vicissitudes: A cross- cultural study of
    sharing and nonsharing. In Y. A. Cohen (Ed.), *Social structure and
    personality: A casebook* (pp. 312-350). New York: Holt, Rinehart and
    Winston.

Cohen, Y. A. (1961b). Patterns of friendship. In Y. A. Cohen (Ed.), *Social
    structure and personality: A casebook* (pp. 351-386). New York: Holt,
    Rinehart and Winston.

Condon, J. C., & Yousef, F. (1975). *An introduction to intercultural
    communication.* Indianapolis: Bobbs- Merrill Company.

Costa, F. M. (1983). Friendship patterns in young adulthood: A social
    psychological approach (Doctoral Dissertation, University of
    Colorado-Boulder, 1983). *Dissertation Abstracts International, 44,*
    1277B.

Denzin, N. K. (1978). *The research act: A theoretical introduction to
    sociological methods.* New York: McGraw-Hill.

Dodd, C. H. (1991). *Dynamics of intercultural communication* (3rd ed.).
    Dubuque, Iowa: Wm. C. Brown.

Du Bois, C. (1956). *Foreign students and higher education in the United
    States.* Washington, D.C.: American Council on Education.

Du Bois, C. (1974). The gratuitous act: An introduction to the comparative
    study of friendship patterns. In E. Leyton (Ed.), *The compact: Selected
    dimensions of friendship* (pp. 15-32). Toronto: University of Toronto
    Press.

Dziegielewska, J. (1988). The intercultural dimension of friendship: A
    study in the phenomenology of communication. *Dissertation Abstracts
    International, 50,* 301A. (University Microfilm No. 8909316)

Elenwo, E. (1988). International students' self-perceived expectations and the reality-shock in cross-cultural encounters. Doctoral dissertation, United States International University, 1988. (From *Dissertation Abstracts International, 49,* 2404A)

Fahrlander, R. S. (1980). Social participation and adjustment of foreign students at the University of Nebraska-Lincoln (Doctoral Dissertation, University of   Nebraska-Lincoln, 1980). *Dissertation Abstracts International, 41,* 810A.

Fei, H. T. (1961). Peasantry and gentry: An interpretation of Chinese social structure and its changes. In Y. A. Cohen (Ed.), *Social structure and personality: A casebook* (pp. 24-39). New York: Holt, Rinehart and Winston.

Fragiadakis, H., & Licwinko, A. (1986, March). *The   conversation exchange program: Foreign and American students together.* Paper presented at the annual meeting of the Teachers of English to Speakers of Other Languages, Anaheim, California. (ERIC Document Reproduction Service No. 274 194)

Furnham, A., & Alibhai, N. (1985). The friendship networks of foreign students: A replication and extension of the functional model. *International Journal of Psychology, 20,* 709-722.

Giles, H., & Franklyn-Stokes, A. (1989). Communicator characteristics. In M. K. Asante & W. B. Gudykunst (Eds.), *Handbook of international and intercultural communication* (pp. 117-144). Newbury Park, California: Sage.

Glaser, B. G., & Strauss, A. L. (1967). *The discovery of grounded theory: Strategies for qualitative research.* Chicago: Aldine Publishing Company.

Goetz, J. P., & LeCompte, M. D. (1984). *Ethnography and qualitative design in education research.* Orlando, Florida: Academic Press.

Gudykunst, W. B. (1979). The effects of an intercultural communication workshop on cross-cultural attitudes and interaction. *Communication Education, 28,* 179-187.

Gudykunst, W. B. (1985a). An exploratory comparison of close intracultural and intercultural friendships. *Communication Quarterly, 33,* 270-283.

Gudykunst, W. B. (1985b). A model of uncertainty reduction in intercultural encounters. *Journal of Language and Social Psychology*, *4*, 79-98.

Gudykunst, W. B. (1991). *Bridging differences: Effective intergroup communication*. Newbury Park, California: Sage.

Gudykunst, W. B., & Gumbs, L. I. (1989). Social cognition and intergroup communication. In M. K. Asante & W. B. Gudykunst (Eds.), *Handbook of international and intercultural communication* (pp. 204-224). Newbury Park, California: Sage.

Gudykunst, W. B., Nishida, T., & Chua, E. (1987). Perceptions of social penetration in Japanese-North American dyads. *International Journal of Intercultural Relations, 11*, 171-189.

Gupta, M. (1983). A basis for friendly dyadic interpersonal relationships. *Small Group Behavior, 14*, 15-33.

Haag, W. J. (1991). Youth culture, socialization, and social structure: How German youth has changed since the Adenauer era. In U. Hoffmann-Lange (Ed.), *Social and political structures in West Germany: From authoritarianism to postindustrial democracy* (pp. 143- 157). Boulder, Colorado: Westview Press.

Hall, E. T. (1979). Proxemics in a cross-cultural context: Germans, English, and French. In E. C. Smith & L. F. Luce (Eds.), *Toward internationalism: Readings in cross-cultural communication* (pp. 120-133). Rowley, Massachusetts: Newbury House.

Hammer, M. R. (1989). Intercultural communication competence. In M. K. Asante & W. B. Gudykunst (Eds.), *Handbook of international and intercultural communication* (pp. 247-260). Newbury Park, California: Sage.

Hanvey, R. G. (1979). Cross-cultural awareness. In E. C. Smith & L. F. Luce (Eds.), *Toward internationalism: Readings in cross-cultural communication* (pp. 46-56). Rowley, Massachusetts: Newbury House.

Heydari, A. (1988). An empirical test of two conceptual models concerning American students' social distance from international students. Doctoral dissertation, South Dakota State University, 1988. (From *Dissertation Abstracts International, 49*, 2419A)

Ho, D. Y. F. (1986). Chinese patterns of socialization: A critical review. In M. H. Bond (Ed.), *The psychology of the Chinese people* (pp. 1-37). New York: Oxford University Press.

Hofstede, G. (1986). Cultural differences in teaching and learning. *International Journal of Intercultural Relations, 10*, 301-320.

Hoosain, R. (1986). Perceptual processes of the Chinese. In M. H. Bond (Ed.), *The psychology of the Chinese people* (pp. 38-72). New York: Oxford University Press.

Howell, W. S. (1979). Theoretical directions for intercultural communication. In M. K. Asante, E. Newmark, & C. A. Blake (Eds.), Handbook of intercultural communication (pp. 23-41). Beverly Hills: Sage.

Hull, W. F., IV. (1978). *Foreign students in the United States of America: Coping behavior within the educational setting.* New York: Praeger.

Johnson, J. D., & Tuttle, F. (1989). Problems in intercultural research. In M. K. Asante & W. B. Gudykunst (Eds.), *Handbook of international and intercultural communication* (pp. 461-483). Newbury Park: California: Sage.

Jones, S. E. (1979). Integrating etic and emic approaches in the study of intercultural communication. In M. K. Asante, E. Newmark, & C. A. Blake (Eds.), *Handbook of intercultural communication* (pp. 57-76). Beverly Hills: Sage.

Kalberg, S. (1987). West German and American interaction forms: One level of structured misunderstanding. *Theory, Culture, & Society, 4,* 603-618.

Kao, C. C. (1987). Adjustment problems perceived by Chinese students attending universities in the metropolitan Washington, D. C. area. Doctoral dissertation, Catholic University of America, 1987. (From *Dissertation Abstracts International, 49,* 1385A)

Kapoor, S., & Smith, R. (1978, August). *The role of communication in acculturation of foreign students.* Paper presented at the annual meeting of the Association for Education in Journalism. (From ERIC Document Reproduction Service No. ED 165 183)

Kapp, R. A. (1983). *Communicating with China.* Chicago: Intercultural Press.

Kim, H. J. (1991). Influence of language and similarity on initial intercultural attraction. In S. Ting-Toomey & F. Korzenny (Eds.). *Cross-cultural interpersonal communication* (pp. 213-229). Newbury Park, California: Sage.

Kim, Y. Y. (1989). Intercultural adaptation. In M. K. Asante & W. B. Gudykunst (Eds.), *Handbook of international and intercultural communication* (pp. 275-294). Newbury Park, California: Sage.

Kim, Y. Y. (1991). Intercultural communication competence: A systems-theoretic view. In S. Ting-Toomey & F. Korzenny (Eds.). *Cross-cultural interpersonal communication* (pp. 259-275). Newbury Park, California: Sage.

Klein, M. H., Alexander, A. A., Miller, M. H., Haack, L. J., & Bushnell, N. J. (1986). Indian students in the United States: Personal and professional issues in cross-cultural education. In R. H. Brown & G. V. Coelho (Eds.), *Studies in third world societies: Vol. 38. Tradition and transformation: Asian Indians in America* (pp. 115-132). Williamsburg, Virginia: Department of Anthropology, College of William and Mary.

Kuo, S. Y., & Spees, E. R. (1983). Chinese-American student life-styles: A comparative study. *Journal of College Student Personnel, 24,* 111-117.

Lanier, A. R. (1981). *Living in the U.S.A..* Yarmouth, Maine: Intercultural Press.

Lannoy, R. (1971). *The speaking tree: A study of Indian culture and society.* New York: Oxford University Press.

Lee, H. O., & Boster, F. J. (1991). Social information for uncertainty reduction during initial interactions. In S. Ting-Toomey & F. Korzenny (Eds.). *Cross-cultural interpersonal communication* (pp. 189-212). Newbury Park, California: Sage.

Lewin, K. (1948). Some social-psychological differences between the United States and Germany. In K. Lewin, *Resolving social conflict* (pp. 3-33). New York: Harper & Brothers.

Lewis, T. J., & Jungman, R. E. (Eds.). (1986). *On being foreign: Culture shock in short fiction.* Yarmouth, Maine: Intercultural Press.

Li, W. L., & Yu, L. (1974). Interpersonal contact and racial prejudice: A comparative study of American and Chinese students. *Sociological Quarterly, 15,* 559-566.

Liu, I. M. (1986). Chinese cognition. In M. H. Bond (Ed.), *The psychology of the Chinese people* (pp. 73-105). New York: Oxford University Press.

Locke, R. J. (1988). The interpersonal environments of students from other countries enrolled at Cornell University (New York). Doctoral dissertation, George Washington University, 1988. (From *Dissertation Abstracts International, 50,* 373A)

Malpass, R. S., & Poortinga, Y. H. (1986). Strategies for design and analysis. In W. J. Lonner & J. W. Berry (Eds.), *Field methods in cross-cultural research* (pp. 47- 83). Beverly Hills: Sage.

Mathison, S. (1988). Why triangulate? *Educational Researcher, 17*(2), 13-17.

Matthews, S. H. (1986). *Friendships through the life course: Oral biographies in old age.* Beverly Hills: Sage Publications.

Maybury-Lewis, D. (1992). *Millenium: Tribal wisdom and the modern world.* New York: Viking Penguin.

Mead, M. (1966, August). Different lands, different friendships. *Redbook,* pp. 38, 40.

Merriam, S. B. (1988). *Case study research in education: A qualitative approach.* San Francisco: Jossey-Bass.

Miles, M. B., & Huberman, A. M. (1984). *Qualitative data analysis: A sourcebook of new methods.* Beverly Hills: Sage Publication.

Miller, J. G., Bersoff, D. M., & Harwood, R. L. (1990). Perceptions of social responsibilities in India and in the United States: Moral imperatives or personal decisions? *Journal of Personality and Social Psychology, 58,* 33-47.

Mitchell, C. (1986). Adult friendship patterns: The implications of autonomy, connection and gender. *Dissertation Abstracts International, 47,* 382B. (University Microfilms No. 8606859)

Morain, G. G. (1986). Kinesics and cross-cultural understanding. In J. M. Valdes (Ed.), *Culture bound: Bridging the cultural gap in language teaching* (pp. 64-76). New York: Cambridge University Press.

Murray, D. P. (1983). Face to face: American and Chinese interactions. In R. A. Kapp (Ed.), *Communicating with China* (pp. 9-27). Chicago: Intercultural Press.

National Association for Foreign Student Affairs. (1967). *American-foreign student relationships: Guidelines.* Washington, D.C.: National Association for Foreign Student Affairs. (ERIC Document Reproduction Service No. ED 018 832)

Oberg, K. (1979). Culture shock and the problem of adjustment in new cultural environments. In E. C. Smith & L. F. Luce (Eds.), *Toward internationalism: Readings in cross-cultural communication* (pp. 43-45). Rowley, Massachusetts: Newbury House.

Owie, I. (1982). Social alienation among foreign students. *College Student Journal, 16,* 163-165.

Paige, R. M. (1983). Cultures in contact: On intercultural relations among American and foreign students in the United States university context. In D. Landis & R. W. Brislin (Eds.), *Handbook of intercultural training* (Vol. 3) (pp. 102-129). New York: Pergamon Press.

Paige, R. M. *The foreign student handbook: A guide to living and studying in the United States.* Manuscript submitted for publication.

Paine, R. (1974). Anthropological approaches to friendship. In E. Leyton (Ed.), *The compact: Selected dimensions of friendship* (pp. 1-14). Toronto: University of Toronto Press.

Parlee, M. B. (1979). The friendship bond. *Psychology Today, 13*(4), 43-54, 113.

Patton, M. Q. (1980). *Qualitative evaluation methods.* Beverly Hills: Sage Publication.

Patton, M. Q. (1985, April). *Quality in qualitative research: Methodological principles and recent developments.* Paper presented at the meeting of the American Educational Research Association, Chicago, Illinois.

Pogrebin, L. C. (1987). *Among friends.* New York: McGraw-Hill.

Poortinga, Y. H., & Malpass, R. S. (1986). Making inferences from cross-cultural data. In W. J. Lonner & J. W. Berry (Eds.), *Field methods in cross-cultural research* (pp. 17-46). Beverly Hills: Sage.

Rectanus, M. W., Humphreys, G., & Spence, H. (1984). *Deutschland und Amerika unter der Lupe.* Rowley, Massachusetts: Newbury House.

Redding, G., & Wong, G. Y. Y. (1986). The psychology of Chinese organization behavior. In M. H. Bond (Ed.), *The psychology of the Chinese people* (pp. 267-295). New York: Oxford University Press.

Rohrlich, B. F., & Martin, J. N. (1991). Host country and reentry adjustment of student sojourners. *International Journal of Intercultural Relations, 15*, 163-182.

Roland, A. (1986). The Indian self: Reflections in the mirror of American life. In R. H. Brown & G. V. Coelho (Eds.), *Studies in third world societies: Vol. 38. Tradition and transformation: Asian Indians in America* (pp. 43-52). Williamsburg, Virginia: Department of Anthropology, College of William and Mary.

Rubin, L. B. (1985). *Just friends: The role of friendship in our lives.* New York: Harper & Row.

Sanders, J. A., Wiseman, R. L., & Matz, S. I. (1991). Uncertainty reduction in acquaintance relationships in Ghana and the United States. In S. Ting-Toomey & F. Korzenny (Eds.). *Cross-cultural interpersonal communication* (pp. 79-98). Newbury Park, California: Sage.

Saral, T. B. (1979). The consciousness theory of intercultural communication. In M. K. Asante, E. Newmark, & C. A. Blake (Eds.), *Handbook of intercultural communication* (pp. 77-84). Beverly Hills: Sage.

Sasaki, G. H. (1972). *Social and humanistic life in India.* New Delhi: Abhinav Publications.

Schaffer, R. H., & Dowling, L. R. (1966). *Foreign student friends.* (Cooperative Research Project No. 5-0806). Bloomington, Indiana: Indiana University. (ERIC Document Reproduction Service No. ED 010 008)

Searle, W., & Ward, C. (1990). The prediction of psychological and sociocultural adjustment during cross-cultural transitions. *International Journal of Intercultural Relations, 14*, 449-464.

Shearer, R. (1966). A comparative study of American graduate student friends of foreign students. Doctoral dissertation, Indiana University, 1965. (From *Dissertation Abstracts International, 26,* 5250)

Shirer, R. K. (1981). *Kulturelle Begegnungen: Cross-cultural mini-dramas.* Lincolnwood, Illinois: National Textbook Company.

Shuter, R. (1984). Naturalistic field research. In W. B. Gudykunst, & Y. Y. Kim, *Methods for intercultural communication research* (pp. 195-204). Beverly Hills: Sage.

Singh, P. N., Huang, S. C., & Thompson, G. G. (1962). A comparative study of selected attitudes, values, and personality characteristics of American, Chinese, and Indian students. *Journal of Social Psychology, 57,* 123-132.

Sinha, A. K. & Kumar, P. (1984). An exploration into the perceived bases of friendship formation. *Indian Psychologist, 3,* 30-36.

Sitaram, K. S., & Haapanen, L. W. (1991). The role of values in intercultural communication. In M. K. Asante, E. Newmark, & C. A. Blake (Eds.), *Handbook of intercultural communication* (pp. 147-160). Beverly Hills: Sage.

Spitzberg, B. H. & Hecht, M. L. (1984). A component model of relational competence. *Human Communication Research, 10,* 575-599.

Spodek, H. (1983). Integrating cross-cultural education in the postsecondary curriculum. In D. Landis & R. W. Brislin (Eds.), *Handbook of intercultural training* (Vol. 3) (pp. 81-101). New York: Pergamon Press.

Spradley, J. P. (1979). *The ethnographic interview.* New York: Holt, Rinehart and Winston.

Srivastava, S. K. (1960). Pattern of ritual friendship in tribal India. *International Journal of Comparative Sociology, 1,* 239-247.

Stewart, E. C. (1972). *American cultural patterns: A cross-cultural perspective.* Yarmouth, Maine: Intercultural Press.

Stover, L. E., & Stover, T. K. (1976). *China: An anthropological perspective.* Pacific Palisades, California: Goodyear Publishing Company.

Strauss, A. L. (1987). *Qualitative analysis for social scientists.* New York: Cambridge University Press.

Strom, W. O. (1988). Cross-cultural friendships on the university campus: Testing the functional and identity validation models Doctoral dissertation, University of Iowa, 1988. *(Dissertation Abstracts International, 49*, 3204A)

Szalay, L. B., & Fisher, G. H. (1979). Communication overseas. In E. C. Smith & L. F. Luce (Eds.), *Toward internationalism: Readings in cross-cultural communication* (pp. 57-82). Rowley, Massachusetts: Newbury House.

The University of Georgia Office of International Services and Programs. (1989). *We're all in the same boat: International student handbook.* (Available from The Office of International Services and Programs, Unversity of Georgia, Athens, Georgia 30602)

The University of Iowa Office of International Education and Services. (1990). *How to practice English on your own.* (Available from Office of International Education and Services, University of Iowa, Iowa City, Iowa 52242)

The University of Iowa Office of International Education and Services. (1991). *Handbook for foreign students and scholars 1991-1992.* (Available from Office of International Education and Services, University of Iowa, Iowa City, Iowa 52242)

Ting-Toomey, S. (1984). Qualitative research: An overview. In W. B. Gudykunst, & Y. Y. Kim, *Methods for intercultural communication research* (pp. 169-184). Beverly Hills: Sage.

Ting-Toomey, S. (1986). Interpersonal ties in intergroup communication. In W. B. Gudykunst (Ed.), *Intergroup communication* (pp. 114-126). Baltimore, Maryland: Edward Arnold.

Ting-Toomey, S. (1989). Identity and interpersonal bonding. In M. K. Asante & W. B. Gudykunst (Eds.), *Handbook of international and intercultural communication* (pp. 351-373). Newbury Park, California: Sage.

Ting-Toomey, S. (1991). Cross-cultural interpersonal communication: An introduction. In S. Ting-Toomey & F. Korzenny (Eds.). *Cross-cultural interpersonal communication* (pp. 1-8). Newbury Park, California: Sage.

Tjioe, L. E. (1972). *Asiaten über Deutsche: Kulturkonflikte ostasiatischer Studentinnen in der Bundesrepublik.* Frankfurt am Main: Thesen Verlag.

Turner-Gottschang, K., & Reed, L. S. (1987). *China bound: A guide to academic life and work in the PRC.* Washington, D. C.: National Academy Press.

Tyler, S. A. (1973). *India: An anthropological perspective.* Pacific Palisades, California: Goodyear Publishing Company.

Valdes, J. M. (Ed.). (1986). *Culture bound: Bridging the cultural gap in language teaching.* New York: Cambridge University Press.

Webster's New Collegiate Dictionary. (1981). Springfield, Massachussets: G. & C. Merriam Company.

Winter, G. (1986). German-American student exchange: Adaptation problems and opportunities for personal growth. In R. M. Paige (Ed.), *Cross-cultural orientation: New conceptualizations and applications* (pp. 311-339). Lanham, Maryland: University Press of America.

Yang, K. S. (1981). Social orientation and individual modernity among Chinese students in Taiwan. *Journal of Social Psychology, 113,* 159-170.

Yang, K. S. (1986). Chinese personality and its change. In M. H. Bond (Ed.), The psychology of the Chinese people (pp. 106-170). New York: Oxford University Press.

Yang, M. M. H. (1986). The art of social relationships and exchange in China. Doctoral dissertation, University of California, Berkeley, 1986. (From *Dissertation Abstracts International, 48,* 1249A)

Yum, J. O. (1988). Multidimensional analysis of international images among college students in Japan, Hong Kong, and the United States. *Journal of Social Psychology, 128,* 765-777.

Zaharna, R. S. (1980). Self-shock: The double-binding challenge of identity. *International Journal of Intercultural Relations, 13,* 501-525.

Index

Activity-orientation, 14, 22, 36,47, 78, 79, 82, 85, 90, 94, 103, 112, 120, 130, 131, 135, 145

Adaptive motivation, 57, 136, 145

Adjustment, 47, 48, 50, 51, 58-60, 133, 137, 145, 146

Affection, 10, 11, 14-15,17, 25,35, 38, 44, 109, 136

American friendship patterns:
  intercultural perspective, 21-24, 26- 45, 65-67, 79, 82, 83-85, 86, 87-88, 89 91-92, 94, 96, 99-102, 103, 105, 107, 108, 113, 116, 119, 120, 122-123, 130, 140-141, 146
  intracultural perspective, 7-24, 127, 146

Authoritarianism (*see* Hierarchy)

Behavior norms, 30, 42, 44, 118-119, 125

Best friendship, 9, 106, 108, 128

Castes, 31-32

Casual contact (*see* Contact quality)

Casual friendship, 5, 9, 24, 41, 90, 131

Chemistry, 49, 50, 67-68, 98, 133, 141, 147

Circles of friends (*see* Compartmentalization)

Close friendship, 5, 9, 10, 14-15, 18-19, 22, 23, 24, 41, 56-57, 62, 90, 131

Collectivism, 30,33, 39-45, 50-51, 55, 61, 100, 113, 116, 120-121, 125, 134, 148

College friendship programs, 3, 70-71, 95, 116, 140

Communicative competence, 39, 48-49, 50, 60-63, 114, 124, 133, 138, 147

Compartmentalization, 15, 22, 23, 28, 50, 92, 96, 99, 133

Competition, 14-16, 32, 38

Complaints of foreign students, 2, 3, 28, 33, 34, 37, 45, 47, 65-67, 79-80, 85, 90, 94, 97, 109, 115-116, 118, 123, 128, 130, 131-132, 141, 143-145

Conational friendship (*see* Intracultural friendship)

Confucianism, 39-44, 125, 134

Contact initiation, 28-29, 53, 56-57, 63, 65, 84, 92, 97, 101-102, 104, 107, 116, 117, 124

Contact quality, 2-3, 47, 147

Conversations, 15, 28, 36, 61, 63, 80, 85, 90

Cosmopolitan worldview, 66, 83,
    96, 97, 98, 112, 115, 117, 130,
    134, 135, 139, 141, 146
Cross-cultural (*see* Intercultural)
Cross-gender friendship, 16-18, 86,
    89, 91, 94, 109, 122, 124, 132
Cultural identity, 52, 62, 135
Cultural knowledge, 48, 50, 60, 84,
    102, 133, 138, 147
Culture, 4, 23, 25, 44-45, 48, 50-
    51, 56, 58-59, 60, 61, 62, 104,
    133, 134, 145-146
Culture shock, 59-60, 137

Discrimination, 11, 17, 44, 52, 136
Duration of friendship, 10, 19-21,
    22-24, 7, 35-36, 44, 50, 89, 90,
    91, 94, 99, 101, 105, 108, 114-
    115, 116, 119-120, 124, 128,
    133, 148

Education level, 63, 78, 139
Ethnocentrism, 37, 47, 59, 65-66,
    95, 146
Expectations, 48, 50, 57-58, 86-87,
    133
Expressive friendship, 12-13, 41
External variables of intercultural
    friendship formation, 49, 50, 63,
    133
Extraversion, 53, 77, 90, 104, 107,
    124, 126, 134

Face protection, 43, 126
Factors influencing intercultural
    friendship formation:
        adjustment stage 47, 48, 50,
            51, 58-60, 133, 137, 145,
            146

chemistry, 49, 50, 67-68, 98,
    133, 140, 145
communicative competence,
    39, 48-49, 50, 60-63, 114,
    124, 133, 138, 147
cultural knowledge, 48, 50,
    60, 84, 102, 133, 138, 147
culture, 4, 23, 25, 44-45, 48,
    50-51, 56, 58-59, 60, 61,
    62, 104, 133-134, 146-
    147
expectations, 48, 50, 57-58,
    86-87, 133
external variables, 49, 50, 63,
    133
friendship elements, 48, 50,
    55-57, 133
personality, 10, 29, 35, 42,
    48, 50, 52-53, 56, 94, 112,
    126, 133, 134
proximity, 10, 19, 50, 64,
    133, 140
self-esteem, 48, 50, 53-54,
    133, 135, 147
U.S. elements, 49, 50, 64-67,
    133
Family (*see* Kinship)
Female friendship patterns, 13-14,
    22, 36, 63, 132
Field of study, 63, 66, 74, 139, 147
Foreign language competence (*see*
    Communicative competence)
Foreign students:
    complaints of, 2, 3, 28, 33, 34,
        37, 45, 47, 65-67, 79-80, 85,
        90, 94, 97, 109, 115-116,
        118, 123, 128, 130, 131-132,
        141, 143-145
    definition of, 4, 47

satisfaction of, 2, 47, 48, 82,
   97, 104, 111, 112, 128-133,
   139, 143-145, 147
Formalization, 8-9, 20, 25, 28, 37
Formation of friendship, 10, 19,
   28, 47-68, 51, 81, 136
Formation of identity, 33, 56
Friends:
   compartmentalization of, 15,
      22, 23, 28, 50, 92, 96, 99,
      133
   number of, 10, 78, 80, 83, 86,
      88, 89, 94, 96, 98, 105, 106,
      112, 114, 115, 117, 120,
      122, 131
Friendship:
   best, 9, 106, 108, 128
   casual, 5, 9, 24, 41, 90, 131
   close, 5, 9-10, 14-15, 17, 18-
   19, 22, 23, 24, 41, 56-57, 62,
   90, 131
   definition of, 4, 8-10, 25, 78,
      81, 83, 84, 85, 87, 90, 94,
      96, 98, 101, 105, 108, 112,
      114, 117, 119, 122, 128,
      138, 145
   expressive, 12-13, 41
   formalized, 8-9, 20, 25, 28, 37
   formation of, , 10, 19, 28,
      47-68, 51, 81, 136
   functions of, 10-13
   instrumental, 12-13, 41-42, 48
   intercultural, 1-3, 47-68
   intracultural, 1, 7-24, 48, 51,
      56-57, 65, 78, 82, 87, 90,
      104, 108, 123, 125, 131,
      134, 135, 137
   programs, 3, 70-71, 95, 116,
      140
   styles of, 18-19, 22, 104, 132,
      135, 146

   values of, 13, 32, 127
Friendship elements influencing
   intercultural friendship
   formation, 48, 50, 55-57, 133
Functions of friendship, 10-13

Gender:
   cross-gender friendship, 16-18,
      86, 89, 91, 94, 109, 122,
      124, 132
   roles, 30, 36, 50, 80
   men's friendships, 13, 14-16, 22,
      36, 63, 132, 139
   women's friendships, 13-14, 22,
      36, 63, 132
Germany:
   case study participants from,
      72-74, 77-92
   friendship patterns of, 26-31,
      77-92
   regional variations in, 26, 31
Global ingroups, 52, 56
Graduate students, 66, 72, 114,
   116
Group membership, 14, 29-30, 33,
   39, 41, 51, 79, 86, 92, 96, 99,
   103, 106, 108

Harmony, 32, 38, 40, 109
Helpfulness (see Support)
Hierarchy in relationships, 23, 31,
   33, 39, 42, 44, 108-109, 125,
   134, 146
Holism, 28-30, 68, 143-146
Homophily, 10-11, 25, 56, 78-79,
   81, 85, 86, 88, 94, 96, 98, 103,
   105, 112-113, 116, 135, 136,
   146
Homosexuality, 14-15, 17, 100

Identity:
  cultural vs. personal, 51, 52,
    54, 62, 134, 143
  formation of, 33, 56
India:
  case study participants from,
    72-74, 93-109
  castes, 31-32
  friendship patterns of, 31-37,
    93-109
  regional variation in, 31, 37
Individualism, 30, 33, 37, 38, 39,
  40, 42, 50-51, 55, 61, 90, 100,
  107, 113, 116, 126, 145, 148
Initiation of contact, 28-29,53,
  56-57, 63, 65, 84, 92, 97,
  101-102, 104, 107, 116, 117,
  124
Instrumental friendship, 12-13,
  41-42, 48
Intercultural friendship, 1-3, 47-68
Intercultural sensitivity, 58-60, 81
  84, 97, 112, 130, 137
Interests, 11, 28, 35, 56, 80, 81, 82,
  83, 90, 91, 92, 94, 105, 112,
  120, 136
International worldview,   66, 83,
  96, 97, 98, 112, 115, 117, 130,
  134, 135, 139, 141, 146
International students (see Foreign
  students)
Intimacy in friendship, 10, 11,
  14-15, 17, 24, 27-29, 35, 44, 47,
  62, 86, 109, 124, 128-133, 145
Intimate contact (see Contact
  quality)
Intracultural friendship, 1, 7-24,
  48, 51, 56-57, 65, 78, 82, 87,
  90, 104, 108, 123, 125, 131,
  134, 135, 137

Introversion, 81, 93, 134
Invitations, 22, 23, 27, 115

Kinship, 9, 33-37, 44, 63, 65, 99,
  100, 106, 108, 112, 117,
  119-120, 125

Language barrier (see
  Communicative competence)
Life changes, 19-21, 23-24

Male friendship patterns, 13, 14-16,
  22, 36, 63, 132, 139
Marital status, 11, 19, 56, 57,
  71-72, 88
Men's friendships, 13, 14-16, 22,
  36, 63, 132, 139
Mobility, 23-24, 84, 89, 90, 94,
  120
Morality, 29, 33, 92

National status, 54, 101-102, 107,
  135
Number of friends, 10, 78, 80, 83,
  86 ,88, 89, 94, 96, 98, 105, 106,
  112, 114, 115, 117, 120, 122,
  131
Nurturance (see Affection)

Obligation, 8-9, 22-24, 30, 33, 34,
  35, 37, 43, 44, 48, 50, 128, 133
Other- orientation (see
  Collectivism)

Permanence (see Friendship:
  duration of)
Personal identity, 51, 52
Personality, 10, 29, 35, 42, 48, 50,
  52-53, 56, 94, 112, 126, 133,
  134

Personality layers, 26-29, 79, 82, 85, 91-92, 100, 133
Prejudice (*see* Discrimination)
Privacy, 34, 39, 56
Private domain (*see* Personality layers)
Proximity, 10, 19, 50, 64, 133, 140
Public domain (*see* Personality layers)

Qualitative research, 7-8, 142-143, 160-164
Quality of contact, 2-3, 47, 147

Religion, 31-32, 66, 81, 86, 115, 116, 120
Rituals, 8-9,28, 34, 37
Role requirements (*see* Behavior norms)

Saving face, 43, 126
Second language competence (*see* Communicative competence)
Self-disclosure, 10, 12, 14, 22, 44, 53, 61, 78, 81, 86, 96, 98, 106, 108, 112, 117, 122, 124, 126, 131, 145
Self-esteem, 48, 50, 53-54, 133, 135, 147
Self-orientation (*see* Individualism)
Self-shock, 118-119, 135
Sex roles, 30, 36, 50, 80
Similarity (*see* Homophily)
Social distance, 27, 51, 134
Social gatherings, 28-29, 85, 89, 97
Socioeconomic status, 7, 10, 16, 56, 63, 96, 139
Sojourn satisfaction, 2, 47, 48, 82, 97, 104, 112, 113, 128-133, 139, 143-145, 147
Spread (*see* Compartmentalization)
Status, 12, 29, 31, 32, 47, 56
Styles of friendship, 18-19, 22, 104, 131, 134, 144
Support, 11, 12, 13, 22, 24, 25, 33, 34, 35, 39, 41-42, 44, 55, 81, 83, 87, 91, 96, 98, 100, 108, 109, 112, 113, 115, 119, 120, 122, 124, 125, 126, 127, 134, 141

Taiwan:
   case study participants from, 72-74, 100-126
   Confucianism, 39-44, 125, 134
   friendship patterns of, 37-45, 110-126
   regional variations in, 37-38
Talk-orientation, 14, 22, 82, 83, 85-86, 89, 91, 96, 103, 112-113, 115, 124, 131, 145
Task-motivation, 24, 56, 57, 107-108, 135, 143
Turnings (*see* Life changes)

Uncertainty reduction, 53, 62
Undergraduate students, 66, 72, 114, 116
U.S. elements influencing intercultural friendship formation, 49, 50, 64-67, 132
U.S. friendship patterns (*see* American friendship patterns)

Values of friendship, 13, 32, 126

Women's friendships, 13-14, 22, 36, 63, 132